THE
NAMES
ON THE
GATES
OF
PEARL

THE
NAMES
ON THE
GATES
OF
PEARL

C. H. WALLER

GOSPEL FOLIO PRESS
P. O. Box 2041, Grand Rapids MI 49501-2041

Cover design by J. B. Nicholson, Jr.

Originally published in 1875 by Sampson Low and Co.

Published by Gospel Folio Press
P. O. Box 2041, Grand Rapids, MI 49501-2041

ISBN 1-882701-32-1

Printed in the United States of America

THE PRODIGAL

He came back from the gray dust
of alien streets and the smell of the swinecote,
back to love.
Two things he would never understand:
why he had fled love for the dark streets and the black wine,
or why,
when he quit the swinecote,
love ran to meet him on the road.

—Lon Woodrum

CONTENTS

PUBLISHER'S FOREWORD

In the preface to the third edition of this volume (in 1903), the author confessed his surprise that The Names on the Gates of Pearl was "so valued by some persons, that when it is borrowed, the lenders cannot get it back." He concluded that the re-issue of the book therefore seemed "to be justifiable on grounds of common morality!"

I am personally grateful that I wasn't placed in such temptation; with a book like this, who knows what I might have done? But the friend who lent it to me allowed me sufficient time not only to peruse it at my leisure but to subsequently use it to prepare this new edition of a true classic.

There are few good books on the twelve sons of Jacob in print, fewer still that lead you, as Prof. Waller does, from the disgrace and disrepute of the patriarchs' early history up to the glory of heaven. The path taken is an inviting one. The author welcomes us along to discover the secret of that process in the life of the believer known as "glorification."

Knowing our own hearts a little, and the damage that sin had done to us, and the slow progress we have made in our Christian walk, I dare say it will overwhelm our souls when we see what our Lord has been able to do, not only through us but in us. Shall we not stand on shore heaven, and breathlessly declare, "Oh, Lord, Thou hast done it! By matchless grace alone, I have been transformed into the image of the Son of Thy love!"

It is my prayer in issuing this volume again, that we all, with unveiled faces, in beholding the grace of God and the God of grace, will become more like the One who came to open, for prodigals, the way back to the Father's House.

J. B. NICHOLSON, JR.
Grand Rapids, Michigan

INTRODUCTION

For whatsoever things were written aforetime were written
for our learning, that we through patience and comfort
of the Scriptures might have hope.
ROMANS 15:4

The Names on the Gates of Pearl are those of the twelve tribes of
the children of Israel. The perpetuation of these names in a city
where there is neither Jew nor Gentile, but all are one in Christ Jesus,
seems to give them an extension as wide as the Church of Christ. All
who enter the New Jerusalem must enter by the gates of some tribe,
and may be said to pass in as honorary members of that tribe. Hence
it appears that each tribe individually, as well as the Israelites collec-
tively, may be regarded as "types (tupos) of us" (see 1 Cor. 10:6).

With this in view, I have endeavored to trace the character and
experience of each of the tribes of Israel in the Word of God. In order
to do so, it was necessary to collect and arrange all the passages
where any one of the tribes is named. And, except in the case of
Judah, whose history occupies a large portion of the Old Testament,
this has been done. The chief difficulty has been to discover the true
spiritual bearing of the history in every case. I have had no beaten

11

path to follow; for I have not met with any history of the tribes which has been written with the same object. If my imperfect attempts may be of use to others who shall succeed better, I shall be well satisfied. That such a view of the history of the tribes is admissible, I think has been sufficiently established. Errors in points of detail can scarcely invalidate the proof of this.

The main object of all that has been written is to direct attention to the details of Scripture history, and to remind the reader that every detail has been given, more or less, for the sake of One Person, the Lord Jesus Christ. "The testimony of Jesus is the spirit of prophecy" (Rev. 19:10). Thus the motive of all inspiration is to bear witness of Him. When holy men of old spoke as they were moved by the Holy Ghost, it was for His sake. To bear witness of Jesus is the purport of the whole Bible. The book was begun that it might be rehearsed in the ears of Joshua; and the angels who came to the beloved disciple, in that revelation which enabled him to complete the sacred volume, confessed themselves fellow servants of them "that have the testimony of Jesus" and "keep the sayings of this book" (Rev. 19:10; 22:9). From first to last, the Bible is a book about the things of Jesus Christ, and the world in reference to Him.

It is not "accommodation," therefore, as some would tell us, to apply Old Testament narrative and prophecy to Him. The Scriptures, He told us, "are they which testify of Me" (Jn. 5:39). However appropriately the prophets and historians wrote for their own times and people, they wrote in the first place for Him and His. But for Him, their writings would have perished. The testimony of Jesus is the spirit of the Bible, which preserves it a living record for evermore.

It has been objected that this way of treating Old Testament narrative leads to fanciful interpretation. But fanciful interpretations are no proof that Scripture narratives are devoid of spiritual meaning. If the teeth of the Bride in the Canticles have been interpreted to mean faithful ministers of the Word of God, must we therefore conclude that there is no prophetic meaning in the Song of Songs? Supposing that men who worked without method have erred, does it follow that there is no true method of discovering the thing they sought, or can

12

we say that the thing itself has no existence? Of course not.

Rather, let us carefully consider and employ the means which we have for discovering the true analogy between Old Testament narratives or symbols, and the life of Christ and His Church. We have precious hints in the New Testament. The fragment of Levitical law, or psalm, or story, which an apostle has interpreted, should be carefully reconsidered in its original place and context, that we may discover by what law of thought or language it bears the meaning which the Holy Spirit has given it. We cannot doubt that His interpretations are according to strict laws of faithful analogy. He did not leave the apostles to the misdirected fancies of untrained thought.

The best human method for the interpretation of Scripture is the collection and comparison of similar and cognate words and things.

A symbol, be it leaven, or honey, or a pearl, or a net, cannot be safely handled without careful study of the various passages in Scripture where the thing is named. A character cannot be drawn from one action. A doctrine is not safely elicited from a single text.

There is as much system and science in the comparison and arrangement of these elements of Scripture as there is in the process by which laws of Nature are discovered from the examination of material things. But the Bible student has the advantage of an express promise of the Holy Spirit—to direct him in the pursuit of truth.

The comparative method is acknowledged to be indispensable when dealing with the words of Scripture. Without the habitual use of the concordance, the best student knows that he has no security for accurate understanding of the original text. But the same method is not less important in dealing with things than with words. Without it we are never secure against mistake. Lack of method will account for nearly everything that is fanciful in spiritual interpretation. It is never necessary to resort to fancy, unless we have absolutely nothing in the Holy Scriptures to compare with the passage in hand. And this can hardly ever be the case. The use of the method which critical and historical commentators already acknowledge to be essential will at least enable us to detect fallacies, and to put what is purely fanciful away.

I cannot pretend to furnish a perfect example of the rule which I desire to recommend, but I have not consciously neglected it. And if any of the following studies should help to enliven the reader's interest in the details of Scripture history, or to view that history as "the testimony of Jesus," I shall desire no greater honor for my work. To set our seal to His testimony, to which we can add nothing, from which we can take nothing away, is the very least we can do. And the enjoyment afforded by the study of the Scripture more than repays the utmost labor that we can expend. "When you glorify the Lord, exalt Him as much as you can; for even then will He far exceed: and when you exalt Him, put forth all your strength, and be not weary; for you can never go far enough."[1]

1. Source not available.

1
THE TWELVE TRIBES

On the gates of the New Jerusalem are written the names of the twelve tribes of the children of Israel (Rev. 21:12). This fact proves their eternity. As long as the twelve apostles are remembered, so long will endure the memory of the twelve tribes. All are now lost in the undistinguished mass of the dispersed Jews. Until the destruction of Jerusalem, all were known to retain their individuality. The captivity of the kingdom of Israel by the Assyrians did not destroy it: the kings of Judah gathered the remnant together into one nation. When Judah also went into captivity, the tribes of Israel still kept their identity. Children of Ephraim and Manasseh, as well as of Judah, Benjamin, and Levi, are stated to have returned.[1] The sacrifices were offered in the restored temple for twelve tribes. These who did not return were not absorbed into the Gentiles in the time of Queen Esther, in any of the 127 provinces reached by Haman's and Mordecai's decrees. Twelve tribes were remembered by our Lord in His promises to His apostles (Mt. 19:28); twelve were acknowledged by Paul in his profession of the common faith (Acts 26:7); twelve were addressed in an epistle by James (Jas. 1:1); twelve tribes contributed their thousands

1. 1 Chron. 9:2-3. Observe this is parallel to Neh. 11:3-4.

to the number of those who were sealed with the seal of God in their foreheads, and are seen in the visions of the Apocalypse (Rev. 7:2-8); twelve are immortalized on the gateways of the golden city. Each gate is alike in everything except its position and the name of the tribe to which it belongs. Every gateway is of one pearl, for all find entrance into the city through the "one pearl of great price"; but whoever enters the New Jerusalem must pass in under the name of one or other of the twelve tribes.

It follows from this that the twelve tribes must be representatives of spiritual characters in God's family, and that the method of their entrance into the city is representative of ours. All the tribes alike were made partakers of redemption, but their experience of sin and of love is diverse. They come from the East, and from the West, and from the North, and from the South. The object of the following studies of their history is to trace the separate career of each tribe in this aspect, to mark its individuality in sin, redemption, grace, and work for God, as depicted in the Scriptures. And the saints of God have an experience no less diverse and manifold than that of the twelve tribes.

2
REUBEN

Reuben, thou art my firstborn, my might, and the beginning of my
strength, the excellency of dignity, and the excellency of power;
unstable as water, thou shalt not excel; because thou wentest up to
thy father's bed; thou defiledst thou it; he went up to my couch.
GENESIS 49:3-4

Let Reuben live and not die; and let not his men be few.
DEUTERONOMY 33:6

No one passage in the Bible will give a complete view of the two-sided character of Reuben. His very name has a double meaning. His course was first downwards and then upwards. He was the firstborn son, but he lost his birthright, though his life as a son of Israel was saved. The father of the twelve patriarchs cast him out from the honors of the firstborn, but the mediator of the covenant interceded for his life. His history is the history of many who shall be numbered with the people of God.

We must first sketch the career of Reuben as a man and as a tribe. There is nothing that we can take hold of till we come to the act for which his dying father rebuked him so pointedly. Jacob knew his son well, and ascribed his sin to utter instability, moral weakness of character. Some have found fault with the expression, "unstable as water," and said that the words employed by Jacob do not bear that meaning. But a comparison of the other passages, where the same or a similar word is used, shows at once that the idea in our English Bible is correct. In the three other places where it is found, it denotes lightness of character. "Abimelech hired vain and light persons" (Judg. 9:4), such as are described by the word Raca in the Sermon on the Mount. Prophets that are "light and treacherous persons, who cause the people to err by their lies and by their lightness" (Zeph. 3:4)—these are the companions of Reuben in that instability of which his father spoke.

Such characters express themselves in many acts of weakness and wickedness; the particular act is of less importance than the root of evil from which it springs. The lack of weight that appears in the character of Reuben, in the story of Joseph, has been noticed by everyone: "Shed no blood, but cast him into this pit that is in the wilderness, and lay no hand upon him; that he might rid him out of their hands to deliver him to his father again" (Gen. 37:22). This done, Reuben left his brethren, thinking by absence to separate himself from their evil deeds, though he was the eldest, and responsible above the rest.

So Pilate washed his hands of the blood of Jesus, who was "crucified under Pontius Pilate" nevertheless. Joseph was sold by Judah under Reuben, though Reuben was not there. When he returned to the pit, to his shock, Joseph was not there! He tore his clothes and returned to his brothers, saying, "The child is not; and I, whither shall I go?" (Gen. 37:30).

How natural was Jacob's conduct in refusing afterwards to entrust Benjamin to Reuben's care, although he said, "Slay my two sons if I bring him not to thee: deliver him into my hand, and I will bring him to thee again" (Gen. 42:37)! What else could Jacob reply but "My son shall not go down with you" (v. 38)? If Reuben could not save Joseph, what was there to suppose he could preserve Benjamin?

Yet there was no lack of conscience, no absence of feeling or ignorance of responsibility. When Simeon was put in prison by Joseph, Reuben was the first to apply the lesson to the rest: "Spake I not unto you, saying, Do not sin against the child; and ye would not hear? Therefore, behold, also his blood is required" (Gen. 42:22). The words drew tears from the eyes of Joseph, who overheard them; but they could not undo the past.

And so Reuben came to his father's deathbed, to hear of the strength and weakness of his character, his many advantages and opportunities, his one seemingly incurable defect. "Reuben, thou art my firstborn, my might, and the beginning of my strength, the excellency of dignity, and the excellency of power; unstable as water, thou shalt not excel."

This excellency that does not excel, the weight that is weighed in the balances and found wanting, is the one fatal flaw. There are resources enough and to spare; natural ability, and the best of it; a large portion of what makes a man acceptable, gives him dignity and influence with others, and a good deal of the force that might bring it to bear; all this in abundance, yet for lack of moral steadiness this excellence is not to excel. This man who is qualified to take the first place shall never have it for lack of application to the matter at hand.

Who has not seen this character and seen it fail? "Unstable as water" is a terribly accurate illustration. The force of water is one of the most powerful in nature, but it is utterly useless until it is confined and kept in bounds. The force must be concentrated or else nothing can be done with it. So the character of Reuben is one which has no power of continuous concentration, and has not learned self-control.

Reuben develops this character in his father's lifetime, and the place of his tribe is thus determined forever. That place may be second; it will never be first. Apart from redemption, it would be nowhere at all.

The history to follow is soon told. The birthright of Reuben is given to the sons of Joseph; and so, when Judah has taken the lead and drawn to himself Benjamin, the remaining tribes are found following the lead of Ephraim, not Reuben. Nothing in the subsequent

19

history of Israel would suggest that Reuben had been Israel's first-born son. The division of Reuben, Gad, and Simeon, is not first, but second, in the wilderness journey. Reuben, instead of heading ten tribes in the land of Canaan, is scarcely head of two-and-a-half tribes in the land of Gilead. Gad has quite as much of the headship as his brother here.

No king, no judge, no saviour of Israel is recorded in Scripture from the tribe of Reuben. The only men of note in the history of this tribe in the Exodus were "Dathan and Abiram, the sons of Eliab, and On, the son of Peleth, sons of Reuben," who insulted Moses, and "perished in the gainsaying of Korah" (Jude 1:11), when the earth opened her mouth, and the whole company went down alive into the pit (see Num. 16). How far this rebellion was occasioned by the disappointment of the Reubenites in being thrust into a subordinate position, behind the camp of Judah, it is impossible to say; but it is an indication of the same lightness of character of which Jacob had complained, that when Korah wanted supporters in his daring insurrection, he turned to the tribe of Reuben with success. And so Reuben and Gad, with the half tribe of Manasseh, after helping their brethren in the wars of Canaan, were dismissed to the borders of the Land of Promise, to a region where they themselves seemed somewhat doubtful whether they would be able to maintain their standing as tribes of Israel and worshippers of Israel's God.

Thus far we have traced the progress of the tribe downwards; now we must observe the turning point. We find it marked in the blessing of Moses (Deut. 33:6), which takes the form of a prayer. This prayer is the salvation of the tribe. Mark the natural end of instability, if it were suffered to run its course: "The end of those things is death" (Rom. 6:21). This is plainly intimated in the prayer of Moses: "Let Reuben live, and not die, and let not his men be few." Why should he pray that Reuben might not die, unless he were on the way to death, in danger of perishing from among the congregation, like those Reubenites of vain and light character who died in the rebellion not long before?

This prayer of Moses is most significant in the salvation of the

Reubenites, for Moses is the "mediator" and" ruler and redeemer" of Israel under the old covenant. It represents the prayer and intercession of the Saviour, which is the only salvation of those who fall, and yet do not die.

The character of Reuben, the first of the twelve patriarchs, is hardly the same as Peter's, the first of the twelve apostles, though in both there is a certain amount of failure and recovery. But there is a resemblance in this—that both of them are saved by the intercession of another who stands between them and death. "Simon, Simon, behold Satan hath desired to have you, that he may sift you as wheat: but I have prayed for thee, that thy faith die[1] not: and when thou art converted, strengthen thy brethren" (Lk. 22:31-32).

Accordingly, we find in history from this time forward, that Reuben has a place and a work. He strengthened his brethren in the conquest of Canaan, fighting under the banner of Joshua till the land was won. After this, the Reubenites were greatly multiplied in the land of Gilead. "In the days of Saul they made war against the Hagarites, and cried to God in the battle; and He was entreated of them, because they trusted in Him" (1 Chron. 5:10). In Reuben was fulfilled the promise to Abraham that his seed should possess the land as far as the river Euphrates. So far the Reubenites extended their possessions in the time of Saul and afterwards, because their cattle multiplied in the land of Gilead (v. 9).

We have one thing more to notice, and our view of this Reuben-character will be complete. From Jacob's prophecy alone we would never imagine that Reuben represents a tribe in the true Israel who will enter the New Jerusalem through a portal inscribed with Reuben's name. We have seen the downward progress of the tribe arrested by the prayer of the mediator, that they may "live and not die." We have now to inquire by what process of training or discipline, under the hand of God, those like Reuben among God's people are brought to a right mind.

1. The Greek word is used in the Septuagint for the death of men. See Gen. 49:33.

It is through the discipline of failure, arising from moral weakness. Disappointment, to those who have the natural ability to succeed, is humbling, and, through the gracious mediation of the great Mediator, the humiliation is blessed, and brings them to the foot of the cross. We have no actual history of Reuben's later life to show us how this was done in his case. This quiet training and discipline is not a subject to be brought before the world, yet it is the history of the new birth of many a soul.

It is represented to us in Scripture by something connected with the name Reuben, and the way in which that name was given at his birth. All these children of Jacob were named from some saying of their mother's, and every name was significant. The name of Reuben alone appears, at first sight, to have nothing to do with what his mother said of him. "She called his name Reuben—i.e., Behold, a son—for, she said, Surely the Lord hath looked upon my affliction; now therefore my husband will love me" (Gen. 29:32). Leah says nothing here about Behold, a son, and yet that is what Reuben means. But, when the name is closely examined, it is found to have a double meaning. The word Reuben contains in it the principal points of what his mother said, condensed, and, as it were, crystallized into the one name. It contains a part of the words "He looked," a letter of the name "Jehovah," and a part of the words "upon my affliction"[2] And the whole sentence, "The Lord hath looked on my affliction," has been abbreviated into Reuben, which means, Behold, a son.

Is not this the history of the second birth of many a Reuben, who at first is no true child of God at all? In the days of his great ability and instability, he is morally worthless, but he is made to feel his weakness. He loses the place that his birthright had entitled him to hold, by his unsteadiness of character, and falls from the first place to the second, though his talents were unsurpassed. Thus he is afflicted, and it is good for him. He is brought down to feel his need of a Saviour. The Lord looks upon his affliction, and he is born of God.

2. In a Hebrew sentence, the verb often stands before the nominative case, thus: "Looked Jehovah upon my affliction."

Such characters as Reuben have sometimes gone a long way with the prodigal; they lose great opportunities and advantages, if they do not actually waste their substance with riotous living, and experience some of the pressure of the mighty famine which the parable describes. Then they come to themselves; and arise and go to the Father against whom they have sinned. They are received into the arms of His mercy with joy unspeakable, and, behold, a son is born to God! "This my son was dead, and is alive again; he was lost, and is found" (Lk. 15:24). This is the true interpretation of Reuben; but, if it had not been for the affliction, the child of God would never have been seen. Not a few among the great multitude will bear witness to the truth of this experience.

Perhaps there is something that answers to it in the history of us all. Who is there that has not lost some opportunity, wasted some advantage, that God gave him at first? Who is there that has excelled, with all the excellency that his birthright gave? Yet it cannot be denied that there are some who carry this line of experience further than others. Yes, there is a gate of Reuben in the golden city, and a tribe of Reuben in the Israel of God. It is interesting to see that Reuben's place among the sealed tribes in the Book of Revelation is first, but for the royal tribe (7:5). Judah is before him, and that is all.

There are such promises in the Old Testament which have comforted men of this kind before now: "I will restore the years which the locust hath eaten" (Joel 2:25). We may feel that in this present life we never can be what we might have been if we had not sadly wasted our Master's good. But they that have known the famine in the far country will feel quite contented if they may at last enter their Father's house above.

Let those who want it have first place, and let them sit on the right hand and the left in the Master's glory; but as for us, we that are of the tribe of Reuben shall be most thankful to be there at all. In that kingdom, and in that city, all things are perfect. Who will presume to mark the first and the second among those precious foundations and those gates of pearl? Only let Reuben live, and not die, and he will bless God throughout eternity for his disappointments and trials here.

23

3
SIMEON

Simeon and Levi are brethren; instruments of cruelty are in their
habitations. O my soul, come not thou into their secret unto their
assembly, mine honor, be not thou united: for in their anger they
slew a man, and in their self-will they digged down a wall.
Cursed be their anger, for it was fierce; and their wrath, for it was
cruel; I will divide them in Jacob, and scatter them in Israel.
GENESIS 49:5-7

We cannot treat Simeon altogether apart from Levi, because their
father Jacob put them together in his prophecy of what should befall
them in the latter days. In the blessing by Moses, the name of Simeon
is omitted, and Levi has a special portion for himself. These two
seem to have clung together in their father's lifetime more than any
of the rest. "Simeon and Levi are brethren," alike in character, and
close companions in thought and action.

But this companionship was not to last. The brethren must be parted: "I will divide them in Jacob and scatter them in Israel." Their
father speaks of their union with strong disapprobation; "instruments
of cruelty are in their habitations," or perhaps rather in their bar-
gainings or covenants.

There was the agreement between the sons of Jacob and the Shechemites, which Simeon and Levi turned into an opportunity for a treacherous massacre of all the men of Shechem (Gen. 34). There was also the bargain by which Joseph was sold to the Ishmaelites, for which Simeon was partly responsible as being the eldest of the brethren actually present at the doing of the deed. There may be also an allusion to the brotherly covenant between Simeon and Levi. But in their union, Jacob declares that he, as the father and head of Israel, would have no part. "My soul, come not thou into their secret; unto their assembly, my glory, be not thou united" (Gen 49:6, NAS).

The second of these two clauses completes the first. Jacob's soul was not with his sons in their secret chamber when they formed their cruel plot; and in their assembly—that is in the larger gathering of their friends—his glory should not be one with them. His glory may mean (as in the Psalms) his tongue: "My soul shall not be with them in secret, nor my voice with them in public," for Simeon and Levi are murderers, and take delight in cruelty. "In their wrath they slew a man,[1] and in their self-will (in the gratification of their desire) they digged down a wall."

The rendering of the last expression is uncertain; but some act of willful destruction which may be compared to murder is clearly meant. And in these two clauses, anger and self-will are side by side: in their anger they did murder; in their self-will they wrought destruction. The word for self-will means also pleasure or delight. The indulgence of wrath and anger gave positive pleasure to the two brethren. This temper of mind Israel condemns in the strongest language: "Cursed be their anger, for it was fierce; and their wrath (the outburst of their passion), for it was cruel (hard-hearted): I will divide them in Jacob, and scatter them in Israel" (v. 7).

Of Simeon's personal history we know little. The first thing recorded is that Simeon and Levi drew the sword in treachery against

1. Not, as has been suggested, "the man." It has been applied to Joseph, and through him, I suppose, to Christ. But I doubt the propriety of the application.

the Shechemites, and slew all the males. When their father rebuked them, they replied with an indignant assertion of their right to do what they had done. He answered them on his deathbed as we see.

Simeon next appears in the story of Joseph. When his brethren came down to Egypt, and he wanted security that they would bring Benjamin, he took from them Simeon, and bound him before their eyes. Simeon was the eldest of the brethren who took part in selling Joseph. Perhaps also Joseph preferred not to run the risk of having Benjamin entrusted to his brethren if Simeon were among them. He thought, with his father, that Simeon and Levi would be best apart.

The Levites were dispersed throughout all the tribes of Israel in the Promised Land. But Simeon was no less distinctly parted from his brethren, though his tribe was not so dispersed. In the first place, the tribe of Simeon did not multiply (see 1 Chron. 4:24-27). During the forty years in the wilderness, the decrease of Simeon was so remarkable that some have doubted whether the numbers have been read aright. There is no mistake, however, as the total shows. In the wilderness of Sinai, the fighting men of the Simeonites were 59,300 (Num. 1:23). In the plains of Moab, they were 22,200 (Num. 26:14), having suffered a decrease of 37,100 men.[2]

Thus Simeon had not only been parted from Levi, but had been more weakened than any of the other tribes. He had been placed with Reuben and Gad, who had both decreased also. The effect of this turned out somewhat strangely for the tribe of Simeon. The twelve tribes marched in four divisions of three tribes each; the second division consisted of Reuben, Simeon and Gad, and the captain of the tribe of Reuben commanded (Num. 2:10-13). When they came to the borders of Canaan, two of these tribes had a great multitude of cattle, and desired the land of Gilead, which Moses conquered before he died. The request was granted. It would seem natural for the whole

---

2. Reuben's division (Reuben, Simeon, and Gad) had decreased in the forty years' wandering from 151,450 to 106,430. The other three divisions had all increased perceptibly. This may illustrate Deuteronomy 33:6, "Let not his men be few."

of Reuben's division to go together; but, for some reason not explained, Simeon was thrown out. He had marched by the side of Gad and Reuben for forty years, but at the entrance into the land, they left him. Half the tribe of Manasseh joined them instead (Num. 34:13-15); and that half-tribe of Manasseh was stronger than the whole tribe of Simeon by 4,150 men. There is some secret here, which has not been disclosed. The decrease of the tribe of Simeon, if we only knew what caused it, would no doubt explain why the two other tribes chose to be rid of him and take another partner instead. But the fact only is before us: explanation we have none.

The other fact, that Moses did not mention Simeon in his blessing, is equally strange. When the Israelites entered the land of Canaan, the Simeonites had no separate inheritance for themselves; they received a portion of the inheritance of Judah (see Josh. 19:1-9). Here the separation from Levi was most complete, though the Levites had cities in every one of the tribes of Israel, and the priests were placed to a great extent in Judah. Yet in the part of Judah's inheritance that was allotted to Simeon, there was only one Levitical city.[3] There is a Jewish tradition that the Simeonites, because of the smallness of their inheritance, became teachers and scribes. However this may be, the isolation of the tribe was remarkable—first parted from Levi, then again from Reuben, and at last placed entirely within the grasp of Judah. The Simeonites occupied the southern border of the Promised land, and Beersheba was in the territory of this tribe.

In time, when the nation of Israel was divided into two kingdoms, and Benjamin and Judah followed the family of David, while the other ten tribes (Simeon among them) followed the lead of Ephraim, the Simeonites were separated by the whole breadth of the inheritance of Judah and Benjamin from the kingdom to which they belonged. We might have supposed that they would have been compelled to follow Judah; but it was not so, for we read that "strangers out of Ephraim and Manasseh, and out of Simeon" were gathered to Asa king of Judah in abundance (see 2 Chron. 15:9-10).

3. Ain, or Ashan. See Josh. 19:7, and 21:16; 1 Chron. 6:59.

Thus far we have traced the fulfillment of Jacob's prophecy, and the curse that he pronounced on Simeon. It might seem that the whole history of the tribe was made up of disappointment and failure. But his course, like that of Reuben, was first downward and then upward.

In the final division of the land, foretold by Ezekiel, between Benjamin and Issachar there is a portion for Simeon (Ezek. 48:24-25). And in the Book of Revelation, "Of the tribe of Simeon were sealed 12,000" (Rev. 7:7). There is also a gate to the golden city over which the name of Simeon is inscribed—a way open for the Simeonites to enter Jerusalem above. But how do such men find entrance into the city of God?

The natural character represented by Simeon is hard and cruel. Men who think they can advance the kingdom of heaven by the sword are here. "Lord, shall we smite with the sword?" asks Simeon, or Simon Peter of the New Testament; and before he has heard the answer, he has smitten his Master's enemy, and cut off his ear. "My kingdom is not of this world: if My kingdom were of this world, then would My servants fight, that I should not be delivered to the Jews: but now is My kingdom not from hence," declared the Saviour (Jn. 18:36). Thus, though the Master is insulted, and the daughter of Jacob outraged, the Simeons and Levis that stand by and see it must not take the sword, or they shall perish with the sword.

"Here is the patience of the saints: here are they that keep the commandments of God, and the faith of Jesus" (Rev. 14:12). "The wrath of man worketh not the righteousness of God" (Jas. 1:20). But this is a truth that the Simeonites in Israel find it hard to learn. They cannot see why they should not do justice, even to severity, upon others. They are austere in their religion, and yet the same character sometimes breaks out into acts of licentiousness, as with "Zimri, the son of Salu, the prince of a chief house among the Simeonites," who was slain with a Midianitish woman by a man of the brother tribe of Levi for his sin (see Num. 25:14).

Of this tribe in Israel are many persecutors of the saints, who think that they do God service—men who take up arms, not to defend their religion, but to propagate it, and those who will put down false doctrine with open violence, forsaking the simple remedies which the Master has prescribed. "And from the days of John the Baptist until now the kingdom of heaven suffereth violence, and the violent take it by force" (Mt. 11:12).

It is always difficult to draw the lines between intolerance and discipline, between tolerance and neglect. But cruelty and violence, especially when accompanied with treachery, are not the weapons for a disciple of Christ. No one ever accomplished by the sword what has been accomplished by "the meekness and gentleness of Christ."

The way in which God deals with this disposition has been clearly taught in the case of Simeon. Separation, imprisonment, and isolation, are the results of this conduct. God's cruel servants find themselves deserted and alone. They are parted again and again from their associates in Jacob, and are at last left almost alone in Israel; their strength is diminished, they are so surrounded by others of a different temper to themselves, and they can work their will no more. Then they are brought into contact with the true gospel. There is a defect in their apprehension of it. They know not what manner of spirit they are of. Like the prodigal's brother, they are angry at the father's ways of grace. Theirs is the spirit of fear, and not of love; and the remedy for them is this: they are first brought low in their affliction, and then overwhelmed with the revelation of the love of God. The Father comes out to them and entreats them.

This method of God's dealing is illustrated by the history of Simeon in a very unexpected way. He had no blessing while he was joined with Levi, no prosperity while he was with Reuben; he only grew weaker and weaker. His natural strength had failed him, and he had nothing to replace what he had lost. But in the land of Canaan he was joined with Judah; and this is the turning point in the history of the tribe.

When we remember that all these names are significant, we will see great beauty in this part of the story. Simeon means Leaving— "The Lord hath heard that I was hated"—and Judah's name is Praise (see Gen. 29:33-35). When the character of the Simeonites had made them hated, the Lord heard it, and placed them in the midst of a tribe whose portion was all praise. Judah was the one praised of his brethren, and the one who had most cause to praise God. The natural character of Simeon is not disposed to praise God, because it does not recognize His loving-kindness. It is all for prayers and fastings and services—"What can I do for God?" not "What has He done for me?"

And how does God deal with such a character? He first shows him that on his own he can do nothing, and then reveals the fullness of what God has done for him. This is giving to prayer a portion out of the inheritance of praise. And in Judges 1, it is recorded that Judah and Simeon went up together; but Simeon must go with Judah first. It is as though "Praise said to Hearing of Prayer, his brother, Come up with me into my lot, and I also will go with thee into thy lot. So Prayer went up with him, and Praise went up; and the Lord delivered the enemy into his hand" (see 1:3-4).

The absorption of Simeon into the inheritance of Judah is what happens when one who has been laboring to serve God all his days with a stern, severe, ascetic religion, having spent his life in doing. Then, awakened by God's lovingkindness, he finds that the work is done, and that he has only to give thanks and praise. When prayer turns to praise in this way, and labor is merged in thankfulness, praise will find a new inheritance for prayer. The true reason why Simeon lies within Judah is then seen. The inheritance of God's lovingkindness is too much for Praise (Judg. 1:3), and he is obliged to give up a certain part to his brother, Prayer.

From this time, Simeon has a place and a work in Israel. Though it be late, yet in the latter days the tribe finds room to serve Israel and Israel's God; for we read that in the spread of the tribe of Simeon upon the borders of Israel to the far south, a detachment of them went to Mount Seir, in the days of Hezekiah, about the time when the ten tribes went into captivity, and "smote the rest of the Amalekites that were escaped, and dwelt there unto this day" (1 Chron. 4:43).

Those last words become very significant when we remember that the book was written after the captivity. We see that this body of

31

Simeonites never went into captivity at all! No; from the time that the Simeonites become aware of what God has done for them, there is no more curse and no more prison and no more captivity for them: they are free forever. God has "broken the gates of brass and cut the bars of iron in sunder" (Ps. 107:16). They overcame the rest of the Amalekites, the last of the enemies. Their instruments of cruelty were turned in the end to instruments of warfare against the enemies of the Lord. And so, after the last victory, the Simeonites, like the Reubenites before them, enter in through the gate of One Pearl into the city. From the closed doors of their prison house of isolation and loneliness, they are brought to see the "open door" before them, that "no man can shut" (see Rev. 3:8). The Redeemer of Israel is their Redeemer, too.

Some of those that have once been cruel persecutors, shall at last meet with the persecuted, where all is peace. The history of Simeon's birth is like that of Reuben. "Because the Lord hath heard that I was hated, He hath given me this son also" (Gen. 29:33). The words spoken to Zion seem to have a special application to such histories as that of the Simeonites: "Whereas thou hast been forsaken and hated, so that no man went through thee, I will make thee an eternal excellency, a joy of many generations" (Isa. 60:15). And again, "Violence shall no more be heard within thy land, wasting nor destruction within thy borders; but thou shalt call thy walls Salvation, and thy gates Praise" (Isa. 60:18).

Can we not fancy these Simeonites looking to Moses for intercession to remove their curse? But Moses is silent—does not even mention Simeon's name. Why? Because there is no need to ask the Lord to do what He has already done. The only need is that the eyes of Simeon should be opened to see it, and that he should learn to give thanks and praise (see Eph. 1:15-19).

4
LEVI

And of Levi he said, Let thy Thummim and thy Urim be with thy
Holy One, whom thou didst prove at Massah,
and with whom thou didst strive at the waters of Meribah;
who said unto his father and to his mother, I have not seen him;
neither did he acknowledge his brethren, nor knew his own
children: for they have observed Thy word, and kept Thy covenant.
They shall teach Jacob Thy judgments, and Israel Thy law:
they shall put incense before Thee, and whole burnt sacrifice upon
Thine altar. Bless, Lord, his substance, and accept the work of his
hands: smite through the loins of them that rise against him,
and of them that hate him, that they rise not again.
DEUTERONOMY 33:8-11

The extraordinary official position of the Levites in the history of
the chosen people does not destroy their individuality, nor make the
tribe less representative of a certain side of the Christian life. In the
sealing of all the tribes of Israel, and in the New Jerusalem, the eccle-
siastical and political difference between such tribes as Levi or Judah
and their brethren entirely disappears.

There was no judge, nor king, nor saviour of Israel chosen from the tribe of Reuben in all sacred history; yet "of the tribe of Reuben were sealed 12,000." The tribe of Levi contained a long line of great men, from Moses down to John the Baptist; yet "of the tribe of Levi were sealed 12,000," and no more (see Rev. 7:5, 7). And as one gate of pearl is inscribed with the name of Reuben, so is there one gate of Levi, and no more.

What have Levi and Judah above others in the New Jerusalem, whose citizens are all kings and priests to God? They need no king, for "God Himself shall be with them and be their God." "And I saw no temple therein: for the Lord God Almighty and the Lamb are the temple of it" (see Rev. 21:3, 22). The kingdom of Judah and the priesthood of Levi are offices in which they are appointed to minister to their brethren here; but they bring no special qualification for glory in the city of God. The qualifications for that are: love that "never faileth;" and "holiness, without which no man shall see the Lord" (1 Cor 13:8; Heb. 12:14). The ministry of the Levites vanish away, and thus we have no need to consider the duties of the Levitical office, except insofar as the office itself implies certain qualifications, and indirectly helps us to discover what the natural character of a Levite was.

The tribe of Levi, though under the ban of Jacob, was fitted, by the discipline of trial, to discharge a most important public duty in Israel—a duty which made Levi second in importance to none but Judah, whose forerunner and counterpart he was formed to be. Accordingly, Levi stands before Judah in the prophecies of Jacob— Judah before Levi in the blessings of Moses, the man of God.

The glory of the tribe of Levi begins and culminates with Moses; and the glory of the tribe of Judah is the Lord Jesus Christ. The relation between Christ and Moses is the relation of Judah to Levi throughout.

Samuel, a Levite, was the forerunner of David, to prepare the way before him; John the Baptist, a priest of the tribe of Levi, was the forerunner of Jesus Christ. And foremost in all the great changes that passed over Israel you will find men of Levi.

In the dark days of the kingdom of Judah, when Athaliah the

daughter of Jezebel seized the throne of David, and thought to have destroyed his family out of the land, it was Jehoiada the priest that saved one child to raise up the name of David, and preserved him in the temple till he was old enough to fill the throne (2 Ki. 11).

The great prophet, who foretold every step in the captivity of Judah, and directed the captives, and taught them what to hope for, was Jeremiah, the priest of Anathoth, in the land of Benjamin. Contemporary with him was the priest Ezekiel, by the river of Chebar, speaking to the captives of captivity, and of glorious restoration when captivity was done.

The leader of the whole line of prophets was the Levite, Samuel. He also first banded together companies of prophetic singers, and trained them to the use of psalms.[1] Heman, Asaph, and Jeduthun, the three leading musicians of the days of David and Solomon, were Levites, too.

Consider the labors of Levi in the Scriptures. Moses who began, and Ezra who well-nigh completed, the Hebrew Bible, were both of this tribe. The second Joshua, in the return from captivity to Jerusalem, was the son of Josedech, the high priest. In the law, in the prophets, and the Psalms, we find traces of Levi's hand.

We have already noticed the prophecy against Levi, delivered by his father Jacob, who set him and his brother Simeon together under the same curse. Both tribes were joined to the Lord through separation from their brethren. Both recovered their blessing through connection with Judah—Simeon by sharing his inheritance, Levi by dividing the chief ministry to Israel with him.

Isolation is a feature in the history of Levi, quite as much as in that of Simeon. The capacity to stand alone, which made Simeon and Levi so conspicuous among their brethren, in their attack upon the Shechemites, proved a valuable instrument for the work of the Lord.

Look at Moses when he was come to years, refusing "to be called the son of Pharaoh's daughter," and finally forsaking Egypt, "not

1. For details concerning this important ordering of the musicians in Israel, see 1 Chron. 6:3; 15:17, 19; 16:41-42; 25:1.

35

fearing the wrath of the king."[2]

When compelled to flee to Midian, by inevitable danger, we find him stepping forward as the fearless champion of the daughters of Jethro against the shepherds at the well (Ex. 2:15-22). Moses in these things acted not only from natural impulse, but in the fear of God. At first Simeon and Levi acted from natural character alone; but it is the same character throughout—a fearless unconsciousness of self, and disregard of danger in the cause of right. Moses for his own part was "very meek, above all men on the face of the earth" (Num. 12:3). It was for others he was bold, and in the cause of justice, not in self-assertion, or for selfish gain. When the fear of God is the ruling principle, this character is one of the mightiest in the world.

This is the material that makes men of God. These men are outwardly and visibly successful in His cause. They are most perplexing to an enemy, because they are immune to fear or favor. It is said that 'every man has his price,' but what is the price of a man who will give his life for a cause which he is not supporting for the sake of gain? That kind of man was Moses, and that kind of tribe was Levi.

Of course there were exceptions—all Levites were not as Moses. There were Nadab and Abihu (Num. 3:2-4), and Korah (Num. 16:31-33); there were Hophni and Phinehas, sons of Eli that were sons of Belial (1 Sam. 2:27-34); Abiathar that turned after Adonijah (1 Ki. 1), and some other blots upon the tribe. But, upon the whole, the Levites were men who would risk their lives for God. He took them for His inheritance, and gave them Himself for theirs. As long as they held by that position, there were none in Israel like them. They were the very men for their post.

The incident which seems to have brought them to their position is found in the story of the golden calf, when the Levites did according to the word of Moses, and put 3,000 idolaters to the sword (see Ex. 32:19-28). Other similar instances will come to mind.

We see Phinehas with the javelin executing judgment upon Zimri

2. He forsook Egypt, i.e., abandoned it and all its prospects (see Heb. 11:24-27). The word contains no allusion to his flight.

and Cozbi together (Num. 25:1-15); the Levite that raised all Israel to avenge his wrongs in Gibeah (Judg. 19–20); Samuel hewing Agag in pieces (1 Sam. 15:33); Jehoiada taking vengeance on Athaliah (2 Ki. 11:13-16); Ezekiel calm and tearless in the day of his sore trial, when God took away the desire of his eyes with a stroke, and made him a sign to the people (Ezek. 24:15-18); Eli holding up against all domestic affliction, till he heard the mention of the ark of God (1 Sam. 4:13-18); yes, and the wife of Phinehas, who made more of the departure of the glory than of her own suffering and loss (1 Sam. 4:19-22); Ezra in his vigorous reformation, after the captivity, going all the way from Babylon to Jerusalem without a guard, with valuable property, unprotected but by prayer and fasting, and then compelling all the inhabitants of Jerusalem to part from the wives whom they had married contrary to law (Ezra 7–9); John the Baptist denouncing the "generation of vipers," with language such as no other except Christ ever used, and threatening the chaff with the unquenchable fire (Mt. 3:7-12).

What other tribe of Israel affords so many examples of stern uncompromising attachment to the law? The tribe of Levi was chosen of God, and blessed by Moses for this very thing. Do we not see the same spirit in Moses himself? See him with the golden calf, actually pounding it to dust in his deliberate fury, and not resting till he literally forced the idol down the throats of its worshippers (Ex. 32:20). Is not this force of character a weapon with which men must not be trusted unless they are men of God? Can we not see now the reason for the diminishing of the strength of Simeon, who had not—like Levi—surrendered himself so early to the work of the Lord? Levi "said unto his father and to his mother, I have not seen him; neither did he acknowledge his brethren, nor knew his own children: for they have observed Thy word, and kept Thy covenant" (Deut. 33:9).

But we must observe that this character, valuable as it is for God's service, has no merit for salvation in the eyes of the Lord. Though constituted the priest and representative of Israel, Levi needed a priest himself—a priest that must be more than man. And thus Moses says to him, "Let thy Thummim and thy Urim," thy perfection and

37

brightness (not thine own), "be with thine Holy One"—that is, the One that is accepted for you, even Christ—"whom thou didst prove at Massah" (i.e., in Horeb, where the rock was smitten first), "and with whom thou didst strive over the waters of Meribah"[3] (i.e., at Kadesh, where the rock was smitten last). The Christ that was proved at Massah must be Levi's only hope.

Let us now draw the character of Moses, the great representative man of Levi, and see what manner of persons the true Levites ought to be. Prophet, priest, and king of Israel all in one—where in all history will you find his equal? "Moses and Aaron among God's priest and Samuel among such as call upon His name—these called upon the Lord, and He heard them" (Ps. 99:6). But Moses is the first of the three—the first priest. "There arose not a prophet since in Israel like unto Moses, whom the Lord knew face to face," and "he was king in Jeshurun, when the heads of the people and the tribes of Israel were gathered together" (see Deut. 34:10; 33:5).

A goodly child even from his birth, loved by Pharoah's daughter in his cradle, "learned in all the wisdom of the Egyptians, mighty in words and in deeds" (Acts 7:22), perhaps even heir to the throne, he chose "rather to suffer affliction with the people of God" and "esteemed the reproach of Christ greater riches than the treasures in Egypt" (Heb. 11:25-26). He was in his element at Pharaoh's court, but no less content to dwell with the shepherds, and to follow the footsteps of the flock. See him turning aside, like a true observer of nature, to consider "that great sight, why the bush is not burned" (Ex. 3:3). To whom but Moses did the Lord ever appear in such a striking parable from nature: "in a flame of fire, out of the midst of a bush," to teach him "the good-will of Him that dwelt in it"?

Follow him again to Egypt after forty years' absence, now so great in the sight of Pharaoh and all his servants that he was dreaded like a king. Yet see him humbly receiving reproof and counsel from Jethro in the early days of his success, and taking his place beneath him in

3. The waters of Meribah always mean the spring at Kadesh, though Meribah was a name given to the place in Sinai, too.

divine worship, "eating bread," like one of the elders of Israel, "with his father-in-law before God" (Ex. 18:12). See him in the noblest act of all, as the true king and priest and shepherd, offering his life for Israel on the mount of God. Follow him as he bears their "cumbrance and their burden and their strife" (Deut. 1:12) for forty years in the wilderness—for he endured as seeing Him who is invisible" (Heb. 11:27)—and at last see him going up for their sakes to Mount Nebo and dying, as he had lived his whole lifetime, "at the mouth of the Lord" (Josh. 9:14).

When did he ever stretch forth a hand against a rival in Israel all the years he watched over them and prayed for them, the servant alike of the people and their God? So God said, He would have destroyed them, "had not Moses, His chosen, stood before Him in the gap" (Ps. 106:23). What wonderful love for the people breathes in all his writings, and yet he himself might have taken the place of them! God gave him the offer: "I will smite them with the pestilence and disinherit them, and will make of thee a nation greater and mightier than they" (Num. 14:12). Yet he did not even take an inheritance for his children. "Concerning Moses the man of God, his sons were named of the tribe of Levi,"[4] neither kings nor priests.

A hundred-and-twenty years he lived for Israel, and when he died, "his eye was not dim nor his natural force abated" (Deut. 34:7). He was ready for the conquest of Canaan even then. He had subdued the giant cities of Bashan, and given three tribes an inheritance never wrested from them until the captivity of the land. Israel held Gilead and Bashan, the "portion of the Law-giver," to the last (Deut. 33:20-21). The princes of heaven and hell strove for his dead body (Jude 1:9), and he stood side by side with Elijah on the Holy Mountain to talk with the Saviour of "His exodus which He should accomplish at Jerusalem" for us all (see Lk. 9:31).

With him the Lord spoke "mouth to mouth, even apparently, and not in dark speeches" but "face to face, as a man speaketh to his friend" (cf. Num. 12:8; Ex. 33:11). Who but Moses first syllabled the

---

4. See 1 Chron. 23:14.

name of Jesus (Joshua) in the Hebrew tongue? He first put together the name that was above every name—the name that Gabriel brought back from heaven after 1,400 years. What can be found anywhere to surpass the sublimity of the Mosaic records? In history, in poetry, in law, in a prophecy, the world has not seen his equal. When his own brother and sister did but open their mouths against him in his lifetime, the Lord Himself took up his cause: "Wherefore were ye not afraid to speak against My servant Moses?" (Num. 12:8). And when he died, the Lord buried him, and raised him again, and talked with him, as though He would not lose even for a season the bodily presence of His friend.

In heaven, on the sea of glass mingled with fire, the heavenly harpers celebrate their victory in "the song of Moses, the servant of God," as well as "the song of the Lamb" (Rev. 15:3). Of all the twelve tribes of Israel there were none like Levi and Judah, and of Judah and Levi there are two glorified members inseparable on earth, inseparable beyond the grave—Moses, the man of God, of the tribe of Levi, and the Lion of the tribe of Judah, the Lord Jesus Christ. If there be a man whom the Bible has put near to Christ, it is Moses. He is the pattern of all earthly ministry—the sum of the priestly character. None were so dear to their brethren, and none so near to God.

In this union with the Lord we find the true glory of the tribe of Levi. "The Lord God is his inheritance, as He said" (Deut. 10:9). The old lawless covenant with Simeon is exchanged for "the secret of the Lord" (Ps. 25:14). The tribe separated from his brother is united to Jehovah, and, spreading himself throughout all Israel, forms everywhere the bond of union between the people and their God. Herein is fulfilled the prediction of the mother of Levi when she bare him—a prophecy of closer union between the Bridegroom and the Bride: "Now will my husband be joined unto me, because I have borne him three sons." Thus she called his name Levi—that is, joined. The true Levites are the men who have been made lonely among their brethren that they may live alone with Jehovah, and so dwell in the families of others that they may unite them to the family of God.

5
JUDAH

Behold the Lion of the tribe of Judah.
Revelation 5:5

Judah, thou art he whom thy brethren shall praise: thy hand shall
be in the neck of thine enemies; thy father's children shall bow
down before thee. Judah is a lion's whelp: from the prey, my son,
thou art gone up: he stooped down, he couched as a lion,
and as an old lion; who shall rouse him up?
The scepter shall not depart from Judah, nor a lawgiver from
between his feet, until Shiloh come; and unto him
shall the gathering of the people be.
Binding his foal unto the vine, and his ass's colt unto the choice
vine; he washed his garments in wine,
and his clothes in the blood of grapes:
his eyes shall be red with wine, and his teeth white with milk.
Genesis 49:8-12

And this is the blessing of Judah: and he said, Hear, Lord, the voice
of Judah, and bring him unto his people: let his hands be sufficient
for him; and be Thou an help to him from his enemies.
Deuteronomy 33:7

41

The tribe of Judah stands on a different level from all the others. Other tribes have their patriarchs, leaders, and mighty men. But the Lion of the tribe of Judah is the Saviour of the world. The fact that "our Lord sprang out of Judah" (Heb. 7:14) makes it impossible to study the history or character of the tribe apart from Him.

Although there is only one gate of Judah in the golden city, and "of the tribe of Judah were sealed twelve thousand" and no more, yet the thousands of Judah stand first among the ransomed, and, but for the Lion of the tribe of Judah, there would be no New Jerusalem at all. What, then, is suggested by the history of Judah in the light of this great fact, that it was chosen to be the tribe of our Lord? What were the characteristics for which He chose it? Or, rather, since He did not choose it for what it was, but first of all made it worthy of this great choice and this glorious purpose, with what character did He mold it for His use?

In this question we are really asking another: "What manner of man did God require that the Saviour of the world should be?" Surely it would not have been the same thing for the Christ to be born of Reuben, Simeon, or Levi. In any tribe He would have been equally the Son of God if it had pleased the Father that He should take upon Him our flesh; but, with reverence be it spoken, if the Lord Jesus had been in any other tribe, He could not have been the same kind of man. He might have been equally sinless as a Levite, but He would have retained the special marks of Levi, even in His holiness, or else He would not have been a real man. We cannot doubt that, being "of the seed of David according to the flesh" (Rom. 1:3), the Lord our Saviour was a true man of Judah, a true descendant of David endowed with all the natural characteristics of that princely family. Even in heaven He remains the Lion of the tribe of Judah, while He is the Lamb of God.

The mediatorial office is found with Judah even before Levi. It is still Judah that draws near to speak a word in the ears of him who is justly angry, with whom the stolen cup of life is found: "Let not thine anger burn against thy servants, for they are before thee as dead men; and thou art even as Pharaoh" (Gen. 44:18). The tribe of Judah was the mold formed for the casting of Christ's humanity. With what interest do we approach the pattern, and stoop down to gaze!

First among the marks of this royal character we may place a certain inscrutability. A really great character is always partly unfathomable. Who has not noticed, in the friend whom he admires and reverences above others, something which he can only reach through sympathy, when it presents itself, but cannot foresee or understand? As men of very great intellect cannot be fully appreciated by any except their equals, so men of this royal nature cannot be fully understood by any who are not like themselves. But here it is not the intellect that is above our comprehension; it is rather the human heart. This was noted long ago as a mark of royalty: "The heaven for height, and the earth for depth; and the heart of kings is unsearchable" (Prov. 25:3). There is an element of true greatness here. This unfathomableness has nothing in common with treachery or dissimulation. It is not that; but it is that the higher and finer impulses of man's nature are partly unaccountable, even to himself. He certainly cannot sound the depths of them in the heart of another; love and trust will touch them, but they cannot be explained.

Perhaps this may partly account for the very great difficulty, which all acknowledge, in thoroughly understanding the character of David. We can fix on many single features in his life, and illustrate them without difficulty; but if we try to put all we read of him together, and paint the whole man, we come to such apparently opposite and contradictory items that it is hard to be faithful to the task.

This inscrutability—the mainspring of the character—is closely connected with another characteristic mark of Judah: a great variety and versatility. What a number of different tastes and accomplishments are found in the tribe! Bezaleel (in the shadow of God), the chief workman of the tabernacle and all its furniture, was distinguished in the wilderness (Ex. 31:1-5; 37-38); Caleb, the slayer of the Anakim (Josh. 15:12-14); and Othniel, the first judge (Judg. 3:9-11); Joab, David's great captain (2 Sam. 24:2); and Abishai, his brother, one of the three mighty men that drew water out of the well of Bethlehem that was by the gate (2 Sam. 23:13-19); Benaiah, the son of Jehoiada, that did many valiant acts (vv. 20-23); Asahel, Joab's brother, as light of foot as a wild roe (2 Sam. 2:18)—all these were men of Judah. Jonadab, also, and Jonathan, the two sons of David's brother Shimeah, what different men! One was the slayer of the last great giant from Garb (2 Sam. 21:20-22), the other a very subtle adviser to David's sons (2 Sam. 13:3-5, 32-35). David himself was the sweet Psalmist of Israel (2 Sam. 23:1).

Ethan the Ezrahite, and Heman[1] and Chalcol and Darda, were men of Judah, whose wisdom is compared with that of Solomon, who surpassed them all (1 Ki. 4:31). Daniel, of the seed royal, had understanding in all visions and dreams, and, with his fellows, was found to be ten times better than all the Chaldee magicians and astrologers in Nebuchadnezzar's realm (Dan. 1). We found the Levites to be accomplished in some of these things, yet men of Judah were their masters in all. There arose not a prophet since in Israel like unto Moses; but there was no psalmist like David; and in the kingdom of Judah were many prophets, and all the lawful kings.

The extraordinary increase of the tribe must not be passed over. Judah was nearly a match for all Israel throughout his history. No other tribe has given a name to a nation like this. The very name of "Jew" meant for many centuries a man of this one tribe.

Again, the men of Judah appear to have been open to the influence of all motives. This can be seen in the ordinary members of the tribe, by observing how many actions of the most opposite kind are recorded. The saying that "the corruption of the best makes the worst" must be remembered here. It was Judah who proposed to sell his brother Joseph, and saw the plan carried out (Gen. 37:26-27). Twenty-two years afterwards, the same Judah was ready to sacrifice his own liberty for the sake of Joseph's brother, Benjamin. "Now, therefore," he said to Joseph, "let thy servant abide a bondman instead of the lad."

Caleb, that followed the Lord so fully and faithfully (Num. 14:24), and Achan, the troubler of Israel, who took of the accursed thing in

1. Ethan and Heman appear to have been Levites by the father's side, and men of Judah by their mothers. They are claimed by both tribes.

Jericho and made the camp of Israel a curse (Josh. 7), were men of the same tribe. It was Judah that maintained the worship of Jehovah when Israel went astray; and yet the first false priest who established idolatry in the land of Canaan—which lasted from the first settlement until the captivity of the land—was Jonathan, the son of Gershom (Judg. 18:30), a Levite of the family of Judah (i.e., of Judah on his mother's side) who came out of Bethlehem itself. Boaz and his household, in the same place, kept the statutes and the law of Israel faithfully when there was no king.

Among the kings of Judah also we have some of the greatest contrasts. We have Jehoshaphat, Asa, Hezekiah, and Josiah, on the one side; and Joram, the son of Jehoshaphat, and Ahaz, and Manasseh, and Jehoiakim, on the other. We have the marvelous and manifold wisdom of Solomon, and the treachery of Ahithophel, who spoke as the oracles of God. Contrast David with his three sons, Amnon, Absalom, and Adonijah: what could be more unlike?

But the life of David himself presents the most perplexing contrast. Look at his noble conduct, over and over again repeated in the case of Saul his master. Yet what could be worse than his dealing with his servant Uriah? Contrast Daniel and the three who faced the burning fiery furnace, all of the family of David, with the four unhappy members of Josiah's family, descendants of David also, who lived about the same time, and of whom the Old Testament speaks with such severity—Shallum, Jehoiakim, Jeconiah, and Zedekiah. Zedekiah was unable to stand against his own courtiers; Daniel and his fellows were not afraid of Nebuchadnezzar himself. All these were men of Judah.

One more contrast, in the New Testament, must not be passed by. The Lord Jesus, who laid down His life so willingly, and Judas Iscariot, who also betrayed Him, appear to have been of the same tribe. If Iscariot be rightly interpreted as Ish Kerioth—man of Kerioth, in Judah—then Judas was not, like most of the apostles, simply a Galilean, but also a fellow-tribesman of our Lord. The one person of whom it has been said in so many words in the Bible, "It had been good for that man if he had not been born" (Mt. 26:24) was

45

likely a man of Judah. The height of self-sacrifice and the depth of avarice are found in the same tribe.

No one descends to these depths of baseness all at once; and the villains of the tribe of Judah are of no ordinary kind. We must suppose, therefore, that all possible influences that can move the human heart could be brought to bear on Judah; so that, where the power of godliness was lacking, there was no temptation to which a man of Judah could not yield. There was no inducement that he could not appreciate—no ambition, or lust or desire, known to human nature, which could not be safely appealed to in his case. From Judah's own family in the beginning, to Judas at the end, the most disgraceful crimes recorded in Holy Scripture belong to the history of this tribe.

And just as in Judah we may find the elements of everything human, so men of Judah could compete with every kind of man. They had the power of excelling their fellows in everything. When did a leader in Judah ever lack followers? What line of kings was ever, upon the whole, so popular as the line of David? All the tribes of Israel separately and singly attached themselves to his person; and his own son Absalom was the only rival who ever seriously shook his power. After Absalom's rebellion, the people even disputed among themselves for the honor of bringing the king back.

One thing more may be mentioned in connection with that part of the character which was noticed first. Probably no mere man ever made the least approach to David in his knowledge of the character of God. Perhaps Moses may be excepted, but Moses had far more opportunities than David of direct communion with Him. This may be placed before all David's other qualities; and the proof of it is to be found not only in his life but in the Psalms. Something of this kind is intimated in the expression, "a man after Mine own heart, which shall fulfill all My will [execute all My desires]" (Acts 13:22). The same thing may be observed in Daniel, the "man greatly beloved" (Dan. 10:11, 19), the Old Testament counterpart of "the disciple whom Jesus loved" (Jn. 13:23).

Another characteristic of Judah may be indicated by the meaning of his name, Praise. In dauntless courage under adversity, the Jews

46

have never been surpassed. The stories of the Jewish martyrs under Antiochus, and of the last siege of Jerusalem, are sufficient proof of this. And may we connect with this undaunted courage a certain joyousness that appears occasionally in a very unexpected way? Seven of David's psalms are known to belong to the time of his greatest distress and adversity. When the people spoke of stoning him, he "encouraged himself in the Lord his God" (1 Sam. 30:6). One verse in our Lord's history conveys the same thought. When "they had sung an hymn, they went out into the mount of Olives" (Mt. 26:30). The night of our Lord's betrayal, which He well knew beforehand, is the one occasion on which it is recorded in His life on earth that He sang and gave praise.

We must now draw the various parts of this character together, and see what is the result. Have we not found in the story of Judah the most complete manhood in the world? Every human capability, every human propensity, every human motive—the heights and depths of our nature—every capacity that man possesses—may be found here. And the strongest must win, if he has skill and energy to use this strength. Judah had the firmness to do so, and therefore "Judah prevailed above his brethren, and of him came the chief ruler" (1 Chron. 5:2). Where else could he be found?

This was true to the end. Who came to the first place among the apostles at Jerusalem, but James (Gal. 2:9), the Lord's brother?—a man of Judah, without doubt. We see what follows when this is applied to the character of our Lord. Here is man in full perfection, and "yet without sin." What can be more certain than that He was "in all points tempted like as we are" if He was a man of this tribe (see Heb. 4:15)? No man on earth need doubt that he will find sympathy in the Lord Jesus Christ, whatever the peculiar bent of his nature may be. "We have not an High Priest which cannot be touched with the feeling of our infirmities;" but one of whom we may be absolutely certain that in all things He was "made like unto His brethren" (Heb. 2:17)—one who fully understands man, knows what is in man, and one also who, even humanly speaking, has no equal in the knowledge of God. It is a remarkable fact that the priestly character in Israel was

47

not complete without intermixture with Judah. Not only were the majority of the priests planted in the land of Judah, but the wife of Aaron was the sister of Naashon, one of the direct ancestors of David and of our Lord (Ex. 6:23; Mt. 1:4); so that every priest in Israel after Aaron had the blood of the royal family of Judah in his veins.

Although what has been said of the tribe of Judah proves its superiority, the fearful instances of apostasy that occur in it shows the utter shipwreck of the finest character without Christ. The character of Judah would not save a single sinner from the error of his way. These glorious endowments have been shown to be useless without the incarnation of the Son of God. Achan and Absalom and Ahithophel, and Manasseh and Jehoiakim and Judas, might all have saved themselves if it were possible for God's children to be born "of blood, or of the will of the flesh, or of the will of man" (Jn. 1:13).

And so we must come to the same mind with the beloved disciple, when he saw the work of the Lord Jesus in a vision, before He had taken it in hand: "I wept much, because no man in heaven or in earth, or under the earth, was found worthy to open the book, neither to look thereon" (see Rev. 5:3-4). We must all have gone to the place of endless weeping unless the Lion of the tribe of Judah had prevailed.

And so, by the authority of this title, we turn at last to the prophetic blessings given to Judah by his father Israel, and by Moses the man of God: "Judah" (i.e., the praise of Jehovah) "thou art he whom thy brethren shall praise: thy hand shall be in the neck of thine enemies" (i.e., shall overtake them when their back is turned to you). "Judah is a lion's whelp: from the prey, my son, thou art gone up"—gone up on high, and hast led captivity captive, and gave gifts unto men. "He stooped down,"[2] when He bowed the knee before His Father, and said, "O My Father, if this cup may not pass away from Me, except I drink it, Thy will be done" (Mt. 26:42). "He stooped down; He

2. I must take the opportunity afforded by this passage, of which the interpretation here offered is little more than a recollection of one by J. W. Burgon, to acknowledge my great obligations to him. To his sermons, writings, lectures, and conversation I owe more than I can tell.

couched; He lay down" in the tomb hewn out of the rock, "as a lion, and as an old lion. Who shall rouse Him up?"

But "He is risen, as He said" (Mt. 28:6). The scepter did not "depart from Judah, nor a law-giver from between His feet," until Shiloh came—i.e., Peace, or Peacemaker, or He whose right it is to rule. "Unto Him shall the gathering of the people be" (Gen. 49:10), or rather the obedience of all peoples. "Binding His foal unto the vine, and His ass's colt unto the choice vine," as He did when He entered the royal city, "He washed His garments in wine, and His clothes in the blood of the grape," when He "trod the wine-press alone, and of the people there was none with Him" (Isa. 63:3). We do not say there is no other fulfillment of this prophecy except what is seen in the work of the Lord Jesus; but that He is the Lion of the tribe of Judah, and the principal personage intended, there is no question.

After this fullness of prophecy from Jacob, the brevity of Moses' words is very striking, but very significant. He accepts the truth of what Jacob has foretold already, and adds a short prayer: "Hear, Lord, the voice of Judah, and bring Him unto His people" (Deut. 33:7). We might add, "Hear Thou His voice in heaven, and bring Him to His Church on earth." Yes, "the Lord said unto my Lord, Sit Thou on My right hand until I make Thine enemies Thy footstool;" and "Thou hast put all things under His feet" (Ps. 110:1; 8:6).

So shall we come at last to the song of praise in Revelation, with which the fulfillment of this prophecy shall conclude. If there was a song of praise when He did but take the book to open it, what shall there be when all the people of God are gathered into the city of Jerusalem, the joy of the whole earth, the place that the Lord chose, to put His name there? Surely then, if ever, the name of Praise shall be fulfilled. "I will declare Thy name unto My brethren: in the midst of the Church will I sing praise to Thee" (Heb. 2:12). And then the living creatures and the elders, and the angels, and every creature in heaven, and on the earth, and such as are in the sea, and all that are in them, shall be heard, saying, "Blessing and honor and glory and power be unto Him that sitteth on the throne and unto the Lamb for ever and ever" (Rev. 5:13).

6
ZEBULUN

Zebulun shall dwell at the haven of the sea; and he shall be
for an haven of ships; and His border shall be unto Zidon.
GENESIS 49:13

And of Zebulun he said, Rejoice, Zebulun, in thy going out; and,
Issachar, in thy tents. They shall call the people unto the mountain;
there they shall offer sacrifices of righteousness: for they shall suck
of the abundance of the seas, and of treasures hid in the sand.
DEUTERONOMY 33:18-19

Both Moses and Jacob blessed Zebulun before his elder brother.
This may be because of the hireling character which clings to
Issachar from the first. Issachar might be described as a son of Jacob
by purchase; Zebulun was a son of his father's love. In the service of
God we know that love is above every other bond. But there is a better reason than this, suggested by a fact in the history of our Lord. It
was something that, when He chose a place of residence for the time
of His earthly ministry (as we read in Mt. 4), it was Capernaum, in
the borders of Zebulun and Naphtali. But there is more than this. The
town of Nazareth, His place of abode for the first thirty years of His

life (by far the longest part of His earthly pilgrimage), was in the very midst of the territory assigned by Joshua to the tribe of Zebulun. This part of the country was never depopulated by the captivity, and many of the ancient settlers no doubt remained.

It was at Nazareth that Mary and Joseph dwelt in obscurity before the taxing called them to Bethlehem. At Nazareth, the angel Gabriel announced the birth of the Saviour, and said, "Thou shalt call His name Jesus, for He shall save His people from their sins" (Mt. 1:21). All this happened in the land of Zebulun, the youngest son of Leah who was the less beloved of Jacob's two wives. If the Christ was to dwell with the children of the freewoman at all, and not with the children of the bondmaid, He could not have gone lower than the name of Zebulun. And yet it was at Nazareth in Zebulun that He was brought up. "Can there any good thing come out of Nazareth?" (Jn. 1:46). "Is not this the carpenter's son"—indeed, "the Carpenter" Himself? And yet it is "by the name of Jesus Christ of Nazareth" that sinful man is made whole. "Neither is there salvation in any other; for it is no other name under heaven, which has been given among men, whereby we must be saved" (Acts 4:10-12).

And the scourge of the Nazarene was before the shame of the Christian. If our lot had been cast in the very early days of the gospel, and we had believed in the Lord Jesus, we should all have been Zebulunites together—at least in name. The world, in its unbelieving mockery, called the followers of the Lord Jesus, Nazarenes (Acts 24:5). Paul was described at Jerusalem as a ringleader of the sect. It is likely that Cana of Galilee, the scene of our Lord's first miracle, was also in the territory of Zebulun (Jn. 2:1-11).

About Nazareth there is no doubt. Can we wonder that this tribe should be placed before Issachar? What a meaning this gives to the words of Leah, Zebulun's mother, spoken at his birth! "God hath endued me with a good dowry; now will my husband dwell with me" (Gen. 30:20). What is this but the mother of Israel speaking of the tribe of Zebulun, that the bridegroom should dwell with her in him?

The word dowry also is suggestive of the history of our Lord. In that dowry we have the root of the name of Zebedee, so often brought forward in the gospel, and yet apparently leading to nothing, because we know nothing of Zebedee except his name. If Leah's good dowry, or Zebed, as it was called in Hebrew, consisted of six sons, were there not, in like manner, six apostles, who belonged to that first company in which the sons of Zebedee were found? Andrew first found his brother Simon, and brought him to Jesus. These two were partners with James and John, the sons of Zebedee. Then came Philip of Bethsaida, the city of Andrew and Peter, and Philip added Nathanael to complete the six. We cannot say that they were all Zebulunites. Probably some of them belonged to Naphtali, but they certainly were the dowry that the Bridegroom brought with Him, when He manifested His glory in Cana at the marriage feast.

Zebulun was comparatively an obscure person among Jacob's sons. Reuben, Simeon, Levi, and Judah, have all something set down for or against them in their father's lifetime. Of Zebulun we hear not one word. He and Issachar were the attendants of Judah in the wilderness. But Jacob in his dying prophecy seems to do no more than point out their future position in Canaan, and Moses bids them rejoice therein.

In the book of Judges, something more definite appears. In the great battle with the Canaanites, in the days of Deborah and Barak, when Reuben stood aloof, and Dan and Gilead sent no help to the Lord against the mighty, several tribes were conspicuous by their zeal (Judg. 5:14-15). Ephraim, Benjamin, and Issachar all did something, but Zebulun is twice mentioned with approval. And "Zebulun and Naphtali were a people that jeoparded their lives unto the death in the high places of the field" (5:18). They came together also to help Gideon (6:35). Two of the judges are thought to be men of Zebulun (12:8-11). Ibzan of Bethlehem was probably a Zebulunite, for there was a Bethlehem in Zebulun, and our Lord's birthplace is almost always called Bethlehem Judah in the Old Testament. Elon certainly was of this tribe.

From Elon we must pass to the time of David, when all the tribes of Israel were gathering to Hebron to make him king. There we find an interesting mark of character in Zebulun. After Judah, and

Simeon, and Levi, and Benjamin, and Manasseh, and Issachar have been mentioned, each with some note of approval, we come to the men of Zebulun, and we read (1 Chron. 12:33), not simply that their warriors were more numerous on this occasion than those of any other tribe, expert in war, well armed and disciplined, able to keep rank; but the last thing said of them is better than all these: "they were not of double heart."

There was no doubt about their allegiance to David, and the motive from which they served. It was not because they "had understanding of the times," and knew that this was "what Israel ought to do" (1 Chron. 12:32), but because they had given themselves heartily to David's cause. They came because they loved their king. This is the same character that our Lord marked in Nathanael with those approving words, "Behold an Israelite indeed, in whom there is no guile" (Jn. 1:47). Nathanael was at first surprised at being known in his obscurity; but he was no less ready to acknowledge the Lion of the tribe of Judah than the fathers of Zebulun had been before: "Rabbi, Thou art the Son of God; Thou art the King of Israel."

There must, of course, be some fault in every tribe of Israel, and the fault in the tribe of Zebulun is not hard to find. The men were faithful, and brave and warlike; but, like many who are thoroughly faithful, they are too apt to despise their brethren, and think there is no one like themselves. We may see this in the question of Nathanael, "Can there any good thing come out of Nazareth?" The people of Nazareth themselves showed the same kind of spirit afterwards to our Lord. They were astonished at His being anything more than one of them: "Whence hath this man this wisdom?" They were offended at Him. And when His reference to Elijah and Elisha among the Gentiles touched their pride, they were ready to cast their Saviour down headlong from the brow of the hill on which the town stood.

So, in time past, some of them had mocked the messengers of Hezekiah who called them to repentance, and laughed them to scorn. A few humbled themselves, but the greater part were wise in their own conceit (2 Chron. 30:6-11). I think the same characteristic may be traced in another man of Zebulun, the prophet Jonah, the son of

Amittai of Gath-hepher, in that tribe.[1] How indignant he was when God spared Nineveh, because it might make his reputation as a prophet somewhat less! These two characteristics of stubborn pride and stubborn fidelity are not seldom found together, especially among the humbler member of the Israel of God; and therefore the tribe of Zebulun can no more be saved without the Saviour than any of the rest. The men of Nazareth only proved their real need of Jesus by attempting to take His life; and may be that by choosing this tribe of Zebulun as the place of His great humility, the Lord Jesus administered the most telling lesson and example that could have been given to Israelitish pride.

Zebulun is associated with Issachar in prophecy, and with Naphtali in history. His position in Canaan was between the two. Jacob said, "Zebulun shall dwell by the shore of the seas, and he shall be for a shore of ships, and his border shall be unto Zidon." His inheritance certainly touched the sea of Galilee, and may have touched the Mediterranean, but the fact is obscure. Nor, again, is the last clause easy, "His border shall reach unto Zidon;" or, perhaps, "his side shall rest upon Zidon." What were the exact borders of Zidonian territory is a question that we cannot answer now. The general position of Zebulun by the border of Phoenicia is sufficiently indicated.

But may we not apply this prophecy to Jesus of Nazareth, the greatest dweller in Zebulun that ever was known? "Zebulun shall go to the seashore to dwell." So He went to dwell at Capernaum; and not only so, but He Himself shall be "for a shore of ships." Who else is the desired haven of all that are tossed upon the waves of this troublesome world? What else but to "depart and to be with Christ" (Phil. 1:23) will bring us to the haven where we wish to be? "And his retreat shall be unto the fishing place;" for the name Zidon[2] is significant. What else was the retreat of our Saviour but that fishing boat upon the sea in the fishing places by the seashore? Where else do we read

1. Josh. 19:13-16.

2. The same root appears in Beth-saida, which means a fishing village.

that He ever slept except with His head upon the rower's cushion in Peter's boat? Perhaps the true Zebulun of Jacob's prophecy is no other than the Lord; and as Jacob's prophecy of Zebulun has a special connection with Him, so the words of Moses concern His apostles, who were partly of the same tribe. "Rejoice, Zebulun, in thy going forth (to fight and labor), and Issachar in thy tents (at rest). They (that is, they of Zebulun) shall call the people to the mountain." And what is the mountain-call but the preaching of the gospel of peace, when they bring glad tidings of good things?

The next clause belongs to Issachar: "There they shall offer sacrifices of righteousness, for they (i.e., Zebulun again) shall suck of the abundance of the seas." Isaiah says, "The abundance of the sea shall be converted unto Thee; the forces of the Gentiles shall come unto Thee" (Isa. 60:5). Thus the allusion is to the multitude of converts that the messenger of Zebulun would bring to Christ, twice foreshadowed by a miraculous draught of fishes from the Galilean Sea.

We see in the tribe of Zebulun the sort of people with whom the Saviour will abide. They are lowly and yet faithful; not of double heart. They are such as will go forth at His bidding to the conflict, and bring others to Him. Their dwelling-place may be hard for man to discover, but it is the dwelling-place of Christ; and they are saved because He is among them. It is not of themselves, for they have pride enough to ruin them. Their natural impulse would be to bid Christ depart. They are too proud to acknowledge Him by nature until they are brought low. Then they become His most diligent servants, and He condescends to manifest Himself to them as He does not to the world. To them He appears in the midst of trouble, saying, "It is I, be not afraid" (see Mt. 14:27). They will see Him standing on the shore, in the dawn of the resurrection morning (Jn. 21:4-11), when He will call them to Himself.

One other thought respecting the tribe of Zebulun deserves attention. It may be called the poor man's tribe. The fact that our Lord dwelt there betokens this. When He for our sakes became poor, it was at Nazareth in Zebulun that He chose to dwell. His first miracle at Cana was called forth by need. The wine had run short even at the wedding—an occasion when everyone who can will provide abundance.

The obscurity of Zebulun's boundaries, of his history, of the very prophecy that concerns him, all point in the same direction. Whose lives, and histories, and abodes, are so hard to trace as those of the poor? It is a fact worth noting that there is a poor man's gate in the New Jerusalem—a poor man's tribe in Israel. Of that tribe are sealed as many thousands as in any other; and the thousands of Zebulun are the most numerous and among the foremost in fidelity to the King of Israel and His cause. The fact that Christ dwelt for thirty years in the land of Zebulun gives it a glory beyond all the tribes of Israel. "Thus saith the high and lofty One that inhabiteth eternity, whose name is Holy, I dwell in the high and holy place, with him also that is of a contrite and humble spirit, to revive the spirit of the humble, and to revive the heart of the contrite ones" (Isa. 57:15). And again, "To this man will I look, even to him that is poor and of a contrite spirit, and that trembleth at My word" (Isa. 66:2).

When Christ came to earth, and sought a home, and a shelter, and faithful followers, it was not in the palaces of the great Gentile cities, nor even in Jerusalem, His own royal city, but in an obscure village of Zebulun, of which no one had a good word to say—a place that had no place in history until it became His home.

> When I am tempted to repine
> That such a lowly lot is mine,
> There comes to me a voice which saith:
> "Mine were the streets of Nazareth."
> —N. ROOKER

7
ISSACHAR

Issachar is a strong ass couching down between two burdens:
and he saw that rest was good, and the land that it was pleasant;
and bowed his shoulder to bear, and became a servant unto tribute.
GENESIS 49:14-15

And of Zebulun he said, Rejoice, Zebulun, in thy going out, and
Issachar, in thy tents. They shall call the people unto the mountain;
there they shall offer sacrifices of righteousness: for they shall suck
of the abundance of the seas, and of treasures hid in the sand.
DEUTERONOMY 33:18-19

The character of the tribe of Issachar is peculiar, strongly marked,
and not altogether attractive. It is useful and practical, but it's beauty
is not so easily seen. The meaning of his name is hire or reward.

His birth was regarded by his mother as a kind of payment from
the hand of God: "God hath given me my hire," said Leah, "because
I have given my maiden (Zilpah) to my husband. And she shall call
his name Issachar (i.e., Hire)" (Gen. 30:18).

It is easy to see the same thought pervading the words of Jacob's
blessing to Issachar. He is described as a "strong ass couching down

between two burdens," or "between the stalls," or "between the sheep-folds," or "between the troughs." It is not certain what is intended by the word used in this place.[1] But the two things here mentioned are a pair (i.e., they belong to each other); they are on either hand of Issachar, as necessary accompaniments to each other and to him. He cannot avoid them, and he has to deal with both. Between them his lot is cast.

Further, it is certain that his position in the land of Canaan was very peculiar, dwelling as he did in a very fertile plain or valley between two mountainous regions. The plain of Esdraelon or Jezreel was Issachar's inheritance. No part of the whole land of Israel was so remarkable in history as this. It has been called the battleground of nations. There every invader who entered Palestine from the north, by the usual road, must meet the defenders of the country, and try and decide his claim. Issachar then represents the people of God in the region where all their greatest battles must be lost or won. Accordingly we find the tribe of Issachar occupying a position of considerable importance in history.

Issachar stood next to Judah in the camp in the wilderness. The only king of the ten tribes of Israel whose tribe we can discover, after Jeroboam and his son Nadab, was Baasha, the son of Ahijah, of the house of Issachar (1 Ki. 15:27). When Ephraim failed in the person of Jeroboam, Issachar took his place in the person of Baasha. His son also succeeded him upon the throne.

The character of Issachar has been made remarkable by the words used of the tribe in the time of David (1 Chron. 12:32), "Of the children of Issachar, who were men that had understanding of the times, to know what Israel ought to do; the heads of them were 200; and all their brethren were at their commandment." This description agrees with Jacob's blessing. The tribe consisted of men who were ready to sacrifice a great deal for the sake of a good position—for ease and

---

1. There are two parallel passages, Judges 5:16, "Why abodest thou among (between) the sheepfolds," and Psalm 68:13, "Though ye have lien among (between) the pots.

wealth and rest. Compromise and tact were absolutely necessary to them. They must be ready to give and take, and to bear much if they would hold their ground. The difficulties of their own position made them excellent advisers to all Israel, owing to the great experience of conflict and perplexity which they had. In their position they were a kind of lesser Israel themselves. As Canaan, upon the whole, was a pleasant land and a great highway between other nations, so the lot of Issachar was a pleasant inheritance, lying between the northern and southern tribes—a battleground for all who were pushing their conquests either way.

The richness and fertility of the country may be seen in the fact that Jezreel, in Issachar, was the residence of the kings of Israel for many years. Jezreel, the seed or planting of the Lord, conveys the notion of fertility by its very name, and the tenacity with which the men of Issachar clung to their inheritance is illustrated by the story of Naboth, who persisted in retaining his vineyard, the inheritance of his fathers, against all the offers and demands of King Ahab, even at the cost of his own life. "The Lord forbid it me, that I should give the inheritance of my fathers unto thee" (1 Ki. 21:3).

Some of the many battles that were fought in the inheritance of Issachar may be mentioned. There is the battle of Barak against Sisera (Judg. 4), which is evidently a figure of something far greater than itself (see Eph. 4, where a portion of Barak's victory song is quoted, and applied to Christ). The kings of Canaan kept the country with their chariots of iron, and "took no gain of money" (Judg. 5:19). When the Israelites assaulted them to take it away, they fought from heaven: "the stars in their courses fought against Sisera" (v. 20).

There also the Midianites and Amalekites, and all the children of the East, spread themselves in the time of Gideon, devouring the increase of the earth—the corn and the wine and the oil which were so abundant in that land (see Judg. 6–8). There was fought the battle of Gilboa, where Saul and Jonathan were slain in their high places (1 Chron. 10:1, 8); and the encounter with Pharaoh Necho, king of Egypt, in which Josiah was slain (2 Chron. 35:20-24). And the great battle of Armageddon, yet to come (we know not how or where), has

61

taken its name of Armageddon (see Rev. 16:16) from har-megiddo, or the hill of Megiddon, a city held by the tribe of Manasseh in the territory of Issachar (Josh. 17:11).

So it is with the Church here on earth. Our inheritance is a land that we have need to fight for, and its protection needs something besides fighting. It calls for men that have understanding of the times, to know what God's people ought to do.

It was in the tribe of Issachar that Elisha, the prophet of Israel, found the prophet's chamber, at Shunem (see 2 Ki. 4:8-11). Even in that story, the hire or reward of the one who received the prophet is manifest. A child was given to the rich Shunammite for hire; indeed, twice given, for Elisha raised him from the dead. It is remarkable that one of our Saviour's three great miracles of raising the dead to life was wrought at the village of Nain, in the land of Issachar, when He stopped the dead man's bier on its way to burial, and bade him arise, and delivered him to his mother (see Lk. 7:11-17).

The spiritual position of Issachar applied to the Church is perhaps best indicated by the prophecy of Moses respecting this tribe (Deut. 33:18-19). There Issachar is connected with Zebulun. The one is the tribe to send missionaries abroad; the other to rejoice at home. "Rejoice, Zebulun, in thy going out, and Issachar in thy tents." But perhaps the greatest sight that was ever seen in the neighborhood[2] of Issachar still remains to be described.

It was on Mount Carmel, when King Ahab gathered all Israel

2. The precise boundaries of Issachar are not easily determined. It would seem that the ridge of Carmel formed the dividing line between this tribe and Asher; but the sea-coast south of Carmel was held by Manasseh, although in the territory of Issachar. The passage which throws most light on the question is Joshua 17:11—Manasseh had in Issachar and in Asher Bethshean, Ibleam, Dor, Endor, Taanach, and Megiddo, with their dependencies. The territory of Asher did not extend south of Carmel (Josh. 19:26), therefore Dor must have been in Issachar. Thus the inheritance of Issachar touched the sea. See Thompson's map in The Land and the Book, which is often correct where other maps fail.

together at Elijah's bidding, with the prophets of Baal, 450, and the prophets of the groves, 400, who ate at Jezebel's table. There on the border-land between three, perhaps four, tribes of Israel was asked the great question which found no answer, "How long halt ye between two opinions? If the Lord be God, follow Him; but if Baal, then follow him" (1 Ki. 18:21). There the power of Jehovah and Baal was fairly tested: "The God that answereth by fire, let Him be God" (v. 24). There the prophet Elijah prayed for the restoration and reunion of all Israel, as it were by a resurrection from the dead. "Hear me, O Lord, hear me, that this people may know that Thou Jehovah art the God, and that Thou hast turned their heart back again" (1 Ki. 18:37). And then the fire of the Lord fell and consumed the sacrifice. Jehovah triumphed, and the prophets of Baal were slain. Issachar had often furnished a battle field to Israel, but never again witnessed such a battle as that.

From this miracle we may well pass on to consider the redemption of Israel as indicated in the history of this tribe. The principle of expediency which belongs to the character of Issachar is very dangerous when applied to the things of God. Nothing is so likely to bring good men and great churches to sleep the sleep of death. The question, "What line of conduct will pay best?" may be asked too often. If halting between two opinions had anything to do with the idolatry of the Baal worshippers, they had reason to repent of it in the days of Elisha, and of Jehu who destroyed Baal out of Israel. This subject bears upon the position of many churches at the present day. They are often a sort of land of Issachar, a fertile inheritance exposed to attack on either side, and the leading men are quite often men who are regarded as possessing the wisdom of Issachar, "having understanding of the times, to know what Israel ought to do; and all their brethren are at their commandment" (1 Chron. 12:32).

But if wisdom of this kind is uppermost, there is great need that the counselors of Israel should be men who are very near to God. They must not be halting between two opinions, living in the deadness of a religion based on mere outward expediency, but as men who are alive from the dead. Elisha, the prophet of Abel-meholah in

63

Issachar (1 Ki. 19:16), asked a double portion of Elijah's spirit to keep him near to God (2 Ki. 2:9). If hire is sought for, it must be the hire that will be given to the laborers by the Lord of the vineyard in the evening, and the reward of the life to come.

The birth of Issachar among the sons of Jacob occupies rather a peculiar place. The twelve sons of Jacob may be divided into three sets of four. The first four were all children of a free mother— Reuben, Simeon, Levi, and Judah—Leah's sons. The next four were sons of the bondwomen. The mothers of Dan, Naphtali, Gad, and Asher were slaves (Gen. 30:1-13). Their children were adopted[3] into the family of Jacob, but they might have been cast out quite as justly as Ishmael from Abraham's house. Afterwards were born four others—Issachar and Zebulun, and Joseph, and Benjamin—all free-born like the first. In the birth of Issachar the free-born sons begin a second time.

He is called the hire or reward of bond service. It is as if one should serve God for some time in the spirit of a slave, and be born again and made free with the liberty of a son after the bond service. This transition is the spiritual birth of Issachar; and the same thing has happened in the experience of some Christians. They have begun to serve God merely with outward form, and from a sense of duty, or for hire, and they have ended by serving Him from love, with the spirit of children. But the change from bond service to the obedience of children comes only by a spiritual miracle, as great as that which was twice performed in the land of Issachar—the raising of a dead man to life (2 Ki. 4:34-35; Lk. 7:11-15). The spirit of bondage cannot perform such miracles any more than Gehazi the servant of Elisha could raise the Shunammite's son to life. He went indeed at the bidding of his master, and laid Elisha's staff on the face of the child, but he could only return unsuccessful, with the answer, "The child is not awaked" (2 Ki. 4:31).

3. Sarah would have adopted Ishmael (Gen. 16:2) but for Hagar's misconduct. Leah and Rachel adopted the sons of their respective handmaidens. But Ishmael was banished in spite of this.

The only way to escape the spirit of bondage is to receive the Spirit of adoption, being born again of the Holy Ghost. It makes all the difference—whether you serve God in order to be saved, or serve Him because you are saved. In the first case, you will give the obedience of a slave rather than a child, and you will never feel sure of your position. Salvation is the reward you expect for your works. In the last case, you will serve Him because He has redeemed you from bondage and given you an "inheritance among the saints in light" (Col. 1:12); and as for any reward that may be given hereafter, beyond the salvation of the soul, it will not be given for our work, but according to our work. According to what Christ has wrought in us here, so will be the place He will give to us hereafter in the kingdom that is to come.

But before we compute the abundance of our entrance into the kingdom, we must be sure that we can go in. "The gates of it shall not be shut at all by day: for there shall be no night there" (Rev. 21:25). But the twelve gates are twelve pearls, and the word gate does not mean simply a gate which moves upon its hinges, but the whole gateway. It is the twelve gateways that are represented as twelve pearls, not the doors alone. And what a picture rises before the mind when we think of this!

Let us draw near in thought to the walls of that city, which we desire to enter at the last. Each of its great gateways, with the porch and the tower above, and the very steps that lead up to it, is cut out of one solid pearl. These gateways are joined to the wall, whose building is of jasper, whose foundations are of precious stones. The structure of the whole is transparent like crystal, and the light within so bright that there is no need of sun or moon (see Rev. 21).

Each of the twelve jeweled foundations gleams with crystal light of some glorious color. The open gates let out a flood of dazzling brightness from the midst of the city, and the purest streams of light find passage through these towers of pearl. Draw near in thought; ascend the steps to the opening, and stand, if you dare venture, in the midst of one of these white porticos, the light streaming on you in front and breaking out upon you from the vaulted roof above, from the floor beneath, and on either side from the walls, of white gleaming pearl. Remember also that it is not the light of sun or moon, but of God Himself who is in the midst of the city; and therefore we cannot but think of it as moral and spiritual light, revealing not the mere outward form of him who is exposed to it, but "the thoughts and intents of the heart" (Heb. 4:12). Which of us, as we now are, would dare to enter, or even approach one of those open gates of pearl? No wonder that there as no need to shut them. We can see at once that it would be impossible to enter without being first washed by the Lord Jesus, from head to foot, within and without too, and clothed in a robe "washed and made white" in the blood of the Lamb. No services or works of ours could win an entrance, or abide such a test as entrance brings. He must be absolutely spotless who dares to cross the threshold of such a gate as this.

The name of Issachar may be cut in the pearl above the entrance, for there is a reward for the righteous; but there is nothing on earth that could buy a passport through a gate like this.

8
DAN

Dan shall judge his people, as one of the tribes of Israel.
Dan shall be a serpent by the way, an adder in the path: that biteth
the horse heels, so that his rider shall fall backward.
I have waited for thy salvation, O Lord.
GENESIS 49:16-18

And of Dan he said, Dan is a lion's whelp:
he shall leap from Bashan.
DEUTERONOMY 33:22

The history of the tribe of Dan is darker than the history of any
other of the twelve tribes of Israel. There is a cloud over it that we
cannot lift, and a mystery that we cannot solve. In view of this we
find the meaning of Jacob's ejaculation, with which he strengthened
himself after the most painful of all his dying prophecies, "I have
waited for Thy salvation, O Lord." The trouble about Dan's history is
soon told. In the seventh chapter of Revelation, in the record of the
number of them that were sealed with the seal of the living God, there
are twelve tribes of Israel mentioned, but the name of Dan is left out.

It is not written that of the tribe of Dan were sealed 12,000. And as Dan is not like Ephraim, obviously included under the name of Joseph, the omission seems absolute. And thus, according to the book of Revelation, this tribe has been cut off from his brethren, and his name has been blotted out. With this before us, we cannot say that he has a gate in the New Jerusalem. Twelve gates stand open there, but we cannot with certainty trace his name upon any of them.

Still there is a fact which may perhaps be allowed to tell against this omission in the book of Revelation. In the city that Ezekiel saw in his vision (see Ezek. 43:1-3), whose name is "Jehovah Shammah," there is one gate of Dan (Ezek. 48:1, 2, 32). There, in like manner, are twelve gates: on the east three gates, on the north three gates, on the south three gates, and on the west three gates; and no tribe is shut out. For Ephraim and Manasseh there is one gate of Joseph, and every other tribe has his own.

The land also, as Ezekiel saw it divided, contained a portion for Dan. It was indeed the farthest to the north, the most distant from the Holy City, but there it was. Unless we can be quite sure that the sealing in the book of Revelation is later than the fulfillment of Ezekiel's prophecy, and the city in Revelation later than that spoken of by Ezekiel, we cannot be absolutely certain that the tribe of Dan is finally cut off. Still the uncertainty is very great. Something in the future course of Dan was a weight upon the mind of his father, or he would scarcely have sought relief from the burden in those remarkable words (the first mention of salvation in Scripture), "I have waited for Thy salvation, O Lord" (Gen. 49:18).

The beginning of Dan's omission from the tribes of Israel is earlier than the book of Revelation and later than the prophecy of Ezekiel. It may be seen in the genealogies in the first book of Chronicles, where there is no record given of the settlements or descendants of this tribe. No other tribe is so absolutely unrecognized there. Zebulun is partly omitted; but the Levitical cities in that tribe are pointed out. The writer actually names two cities which belonged to the Levites in Dan's inheritance, but does not say that they were in Dan, as if he would not admit to the existence of the tribe. It has been suggested

68

that the Danites were extinct when the Chronicles were written, after the return from Babylon; but it is more likely that they were blotted out of the records for the persistent idolatry that clung to some of them from first to last.

This brings as to the chief fact recorded against them in the early days of Israel's history in the land of Canaan. In Judges 18:11, we find 600 men of the family of the Danites going up to possess their inheritance in the far north. They came to a house where there were idols, and we read that they took them for their own. This is the great scandal connected with their history. In the beginning of the estab-lishment of Israel, the Danites established idolatry among them-selves (Judg. 18:11-31).

No wonder that Jeroboam the son of Nebat, who made Israel to sin, set up a golden calf in that Danite city where there was a place of idol worship already existing (see 1 Ki. 12:25-30). The Danites were first in that iniquity. They, even before Jeroboam, had been guilty of making Israel to sin. The descendants of Jonathan, the apos-tate Levite, were priests among them "until the day of the captivity of the land" (Judg. 18:30). And they had Micah's graven image (v. 31) all the while the house of God was in Shiloh.[1]

We ought, however, to observe that this was a separate section, not the whole tribe. The idolatrous Danites lived in the far north, but the first part of Dan's inheritance was in the neighborhood of Joppa, on the borders of the Philistine country between Judah and the sea. Accordingly, when Israel was to be delivered from Philistine oppres-sion, a judge of the tribe of Dan was chosen to begin the work. And the name of Samson alone would make the tribe of Dan famous for evermore. And as it is specially recorded that the Danites went down to the sea in ships, and did business, in great waters—they being in possession of the principal seaport in Israel's dominion—it is impos-sible to say whether the remnant of this tribe may have penetrated, or from what country they might be recovered by Him who knows all.

1. The captivity alluded to here is thought to be the "desolation of Shiloh" of which we have no direct history.

The Danites of Joppa and its borders are under no special mark of condemnation. They may yet continue in their place in Israel, and reappear in the fulfillment of Ezekiel's prophecy in the latter days.

The prophecy of Jacob concerning Dan has certainly a twofold character. The first words are a promise of dignity for the tribe: "Dan shall judge his people as one of the scepters of Israel." The word rendered tribe means also a scepter it is the same used of Judah (Gen. 49:10). And Dan did indeed hold a scepter in Israel. This tribe was by far the largest in the wilderness after Judah. Judah led the van; Dan was captain of the fourth division, and brought up the rear (Num. 1–2).

When two chief workmen were selected to build the tabernacle and prepare all its furniture, the first was Bezaleel of the tribe of Judah, the second was Aholiab of the tribe of Dan (see Ex. 31:1-11). The chief workman of the temple of Solomon was also connected, through his mother, with the tribes of Naphtali and Dan (see 1 Ki. 4:6; 5:14). No man among all the judges did so much for Israel single-handed as Samson the great Danite. His birth was announced by the Angel of the Covenant, whose name is Wonderful[2] (i.e., by the Son of God Himself).

No other persons in the Holy Scriptures were thus honored, except the two sons of Abraham, yet side by side with all this is the other half of the picture. The man stoned in the wilderness for blasphemy was half Egyptian and half an Israelite, of the tribe of Dan (see Lev. 24:10-16). Samson himself has left such a doubtful character behind him that many will not allow that he was a man of God, although he saved Israel by faith (Heb. 11:32). And he did more for the people by his death than by his life (Judg. 16:30). We see great strength and ability in the Danites, but the power is often wasted and misused.

It is remarkable that Jacob compares this tribe to a serpent, and Moses to a lion. Both these comparisons appear to be unfavorable. There is the cunning of the serpent and the strength of the lion in the tribe; but that cunning appears to be used against God's people, so as

2. In the KJV the word is translated secret. See Judg. 13:18; Isa. 9:6.

to put a stumbling-block, a temptation to idolatry, in their way; and the lion's whelp of whom Moses speaks is not like the Lion of the tribe of Judah, but "he shall leap from Bashan." That may refer to the position of the northern colony, though it was almost, if not quite, out of Bashan; or the meaning may be spiritual, and, if so, the associations with the hill of Bashan in Scripture are seldom good. The "bulls of Bashan" are taken, in Psalm 22:12, to stand for the enemies of the Lord. The "kine [cows] of Bashan" occupy a similar place in prophecy (Amos 4:1); and in one place "the hill of Bashan" and "the hill of God" seem to be contrasted with each other and opposed (Ps. 68:15).

From the comparison of Dan to a serpent, it was said in ancient times that Antichrist would come from him. That notion is a somewhat strange one, but it shows the thoughts that have been suggested by what is written of the tribe. The "lion and adder" are both names of "our adversary, the devil" (1 Pet. 5:8), and in tempting their brethren to idolatry some of the Danites acted the devil's part. We cannot wonder that the tribe is rejected in Scripture when we remember the penalties threatened by our Saviour against those who cause their brethren to offend.

There is nothing attractive in dwelling longer on this tribe. Uncertainty upon the great question of redemption mars everything else. To see admirable qualities in anyone only pains us when we cannot be certain that he is redeemed of the Lord. The redemption of this tribe is left doubtful; and what is the value of his exploits if he is at length to be banished from the Israel of God?

In several instances we have found a note of redemption connected with the birth of the patriarchs who headed the twelve tribes. The birth of Dan arises out of jealousy and inordinate desire. When Rachel saw she bare Jacob no children, she envied her sister, and said to Jacob, "Give me children, or else I die" (Gen. 30:1). Her strong desire to be a mother in Israel led her to take the same means which brought about the birth of Ishmael in Abraham's house. Dan was the Ishmael of Jacob's family—the chief among the sons of the bondwomen, born after the flesh.

There seems to be a kind of retribution in his history for his mother's lack of submission to the will of God.[3] They who will have their own way shall sometimes have it to their own sorrow and loss. When we contrast Rachel's intense and undisciplined eagerness for this son with the final uncertainty of his place in Israel, we cannot but be impressed with the thought how essential it is in all things to ask according to the will of God. The well-known stories of persons who set their hearts upon what God had not given them for themselves or their children, and murmured until they gained it, and then found themselves far more unhappy than before, come to mind here.

A further meaning is thus suggested for the words that Jacob added to his prophecy of Dan: "I have waited for Thy salvation, O Lord" (Gen. 49:18). But the one great fact suggested by the history of the Danites, which we cannot escape, is this: "They are not all Israel which are of Israel" (Rom. 9:6). As there was one among the twelve apostles, so there was one among the twelve tribes for whom, though his birth was expected with such eagerness, it may have been better that he should not have been born. The uncertainty that hangs over the case does not make it less painful.

There is no subject in which Holy Scripture is so silent as that of comfort to those who mourn for their brethren, of whose inheritance in the unseen world they cannot be sure. What can be more painful than the thought of separation, in the life to come, from anyone whom we cling to here? I have often wondered why Scripture is so silent concerning the most painful thing that can possibly happen to a child of God. But I have never seen anything that would touch the subject except these words of Jacob, spoken as the future history of Dan passed before him, "I have waited for Thy salvation, O Lord."

The future judgment of any who are dear to us is too terrible to discuss; but, terrible as it is, the anxiety is in no way mitigated by the dangerous attempts, now so common, to destroy the doctrine of future punishment as it stands in the Word of God. Say, if you will, that eternity is a thing of which men can form no adequate notion—

3. "God hath judged me, and hath also heard my voice, and given me a son" (Gen. 30:6).

that you are content to leave it with Him who loved us "with an ever-lasting love" (Jer. 31:3)—who "has no pleasure in the death of him that dieth" (Ezek. 18:32), though He declares that He will bid His enemies depart from Him accursed "into everlasting punishment" at the judgment of the great day (Mt. 25:46).

Go as far as Jacob's words may permit you, and say you will wait and see what shall happen to the serpent and all his children, and the utmost that God's salvation will ever bring. Say, if you will, "I have waited, and I will wait, and pronounce no judgment upon anyone until I see how it shall go with us, waiting for Thy salvation, O Lord." But, of all dangerous things in the world, avoid the danger of explaining away the Scripture, and listening to the audacious theories of those who would clear up all the dark places of the Word of God. "Thy righteousness is like the strong mountains; Thy judgments are a great deep" (Ps. 36:6). "I will wait for Thy salvation." "How excellent is Thy [mercy], O God; therefore the children of men put their trust under the shadow of Thy wings. They shall be abundantly satisfied with the fatness of Thy house, and Thou shall make them drink of the river of Thy pleasures" (Ps. 36:7-8).

The intense light and purity of the gate, which we must pass to enter the New Jerusalem, should make it clear to us that there is no way to enter, except to be washed in the blood of Jesus. Of everyone who has "washed his robe and made it white in the blood of the Lamb" (Rev. 7:14), we can be certain that he will "enter in through the gates into the city" (22:14). Of everyone whose sins are not washed away by the blood, we can be just as certain that he will not be in the great multitude that shall "walk with Him in white" (3:4).

Dan judged his people as one of the scepters of Israel, and he was like Judah, a lion's whelp; but if the seal of God is not upon the forehead, what can the glory of man do to save him?

> None other Lamb! none other name!
> None other hope in heaven, or earth, or sea!
> None other hiding-place for sin and shame!
> None beside Thee!   —C. ROSSETTI

9
NAPHTALI

Naphtali is a hind let loose: he giveth goodly words.
GENESIS 49:21

And of Naphtali he said, O Naphtali, satisfied with favor, and full
with the blessing of the Lord: possess thou the west and the south.
DEUTERONOMY 33:23

The tribe of Naphtali is remarkable in Israel for the changes and
vicissitudes of his career. Dan and Naphtali were brothers, sons of
one mother. They marched together in the Exodus; but, if we may
judge by the prophecies which describe them, their characters must
have been totally unlike. What could Dan—"the serpent and adder in
the path," "the lion's whelp" leaping from the hill of Bashan—have
in common with the gentle "hind," sent forth to be the giver of goodly words? We are not surprised, therefore, to find Naphtali joined in
history with Zebulun, and with Manasseh among the sealed tribes of
Israel at the last.

The prophecies of Jacob and Moses respecting Naphtali both
seem to have a spiritual bearing. "The giver of goodly words" is generally admitted to be a preacher of the gospel. The tribe "satisfied

75

with favor, and full with the blessing of the Lord," may well go forth to "possess the west and the south,"—the most distant regions of the earth—for Him.

The separation between Dan and Naphtali is remarkable, because in most instances the natural ties of Jacob's family have been finally preserved. If broken for a season, they have been restored forever. Dan and Naphtali were, however, parted in prophecy and history and final destiny. Was the Danite conquest of Laish an attempt on the part of Dan to rejoin his brother, by taking a second inheritance nearer to him? If it was, the manner of the attempt is noteworthy, as exhibiting a diversity of character which would have parted the brothers in any case, however near neighbors they might be. From the beginning, Naphtali was "valiant for the truth upon the earth" (Jer. 9:3); and his brother Dan zealous for idolatry.

That first occasion when the tribe of Naphtali took a distant position in Israel was in the war with the Canaanites under Barak. When Jabin and Sisera, with their 900 chariots of iron, had mightily oppressed the children of Israel for twenty years, the Lord God of Israel commanded that 10,000 men of the children of Naphtali and the children of Zebulun should go up with Barak to Mount Tabor, and He would deliver the enemies into their hand (see Judg. 4:6). On that day, when Reuben, and Dan, and Gilead, and Asher, lent no hand to smite the oppressors of Israel, "Zebulun and Naphtali were a people that jeoparded their lives unto the death in the high places of the field" (5:18). Barak, the leader in that great battle, was a man of Kadesh-Naphtali, a town which was at once the center of Galilee and the sacred stronghold of the tribe. The song of Deborah and Barak (5:1-31) is a sufficient evidence of the tremendous importance of that desperate struggle, and the impression which it left on the national mind.

By the victory of that day the fame of Naphtali was established. The store cities of Naphtali were important strongholds of northern Israel throughout history, and are specially mentioned in the wars with Damascus and Assyria, being among the most northern outposts of Israel.

But it is the words of Isaiah, cited in the Gospel of Matthew, that most engage our interest concerning the tribe. When the Saviour of the world chose a place for the home of His earthly ministry, it was "Capernaum, in the borders of Zebulun and Naphtali." There "the people that sat in darkness saw great light" (Mt. 4:13, 16); and the name of Galileans, so inseparable from the apostles, itself denotes the members of the circle about Kedesh-Naphtali, which was called Kedesh in Galilee—i.e., in the circle—as early as the time of Joshua (Josh. 20:1).

Men and angels agreed in calling the apostles "men of Galilee"— i.e., men of the circle of Kedesh—the holy circle, the company of "the Holy One of Israel." "Ye men of Galilee, why stand ye gazing up into heaven?" (Acts 1:11). He that was the Center of your hopes and affections here shall come again. And on the day of Pentecost, when the Spirit of Holiness descended to "give the goodly words" of the gospel, they that had heard it said, "Behold, are not all these which speak Galileans?" (Acts 2:7).

We may notice here the peculiar mention of Zebulun and Naphtali in the Pentecostal Psalm (Ps. 68). There "princes of Zebulun and princes of Naphtali" are coupled with "princes of Judah" and "their ruler Benjamin" (v. 27). It is a striking proof of the honor attained by Zebulun and Naphtali in the time of David that they should thus be placed on a level with the two royal tribes; and the fulfillment of this honorable prediction in the times of the gospel is too plain to be over-looked. The eighteenth verse of the Psalm describes the ascension of our Lord, with the outpouring of the Holy Spirit. In verses 26 and 27, mention is made of the men "of the fountain of Israel" (i.e., of that nation) who "blessed the Lord in the congregations," when the Spirit had been poured out. "There is little Benjamin, their Ruler," in the person of Paul, not a whit behind the very chiefest apostles, for he "labored more abundantly than they all" (1 Cor. 15:10). James, Cephas, and John, who seemed to be pillars, in conference added nothing to him. Peter, always named first among the twelve, was even rebuked by Paul, and blamed.

In those days the apostles at Jerusalem were the true council of

Israel, a council that the Sanhedrin itself was not able to withstand; but they were from the first a company of Galileans, "princes of Zebulun and princes of Naphtali" (Ps. 68:27), when they dwelt at Capernaum with the Lord.

It is generally admitted that Jacob's blessing upon Naphtali was a prophecy of missionary work: "Naphtali is a hind let loose; the giver of goodly words." The name of Naphtali is itself descriptive of conflict. "With great wrestlings, wrestlings of God," said Rachel, "I have wrestled with my sister, and have prevailed" (Gen. 30:8). Dan was the outburst of human passion. Naphtali is the wrestling of his mother that sons may be born into the Israel of God. What great conflict had the New Testament "princes of Naphtali and Zebulun," "travailing in birth" till Christ should be formed in the Gentiles to whom they preached (Gal. 4:19)!

"The hind let loose," or sent forth, is a figure of the messengers whose feet are "beautiful...upon the mountains" (Isa. 52:7) to publish the gospel of peace and bring glad tidings of good things. "The giver of goodly words" is an expression that scarcely needs explanation. "Lord, to whom shall we go? Thou hast the words of eternal life" (Jn. 6:68). "I have given unto them the words which Thou gavest Me, and they have received them" (Jn. 17:8). They "published the word of the Lord" (Ps. 68:11).

The "hind let loose"—Ayalah Sh'loochah—may be itself a figure of Jesus Christ. The 22nd Psalm, which speaks so much of Him, is a song upon Ayelet ha Shahar, the "hind of the morning." The Messiah in all the tribes of Israel is their real glory. They are only true sons of Israel insofar as He is in them and they in Him.

The "goodly words" (words of beauty) are called by a name that is closely connected with the trumpet of the jubilee, that sounded to proclaim liberty and forgiveness on the Day of Atonement throughout all the land. Forgiveness is the keynote of the gospel, which proclaims "liberty to the captives, and the opening of the prison to them that are bound" (Isa. 61:1). Thus the prophecy of Jacob foretold the character and office of Naphtali. Moses described the blessing which should qualify him to fulfill his work; and of Naphtali he said, "O

Naphtali, satisfied with favor, and full with the blessing of the Lord, possess thou the west and the south" (Deut. 33:23).

The favor here spoken of is the good pleasure and delight which God the Father has in His Son Jesus Christ, and the acceptance of sinners through Him. With this favor, Naphtali is satisfied. It is a strong expression. It signifies not merely that the men of Naphtali are accepted for Christ's sake, but that they feed continually on the delight of that acceptance, and feast on it until they are satisfied and full with the blessing of the Lord. Then the full heart overflows to tell others, and they begin to give forth the goodly words.

Their feet are like hind's feet, as swift as the roes on the mountains. They go forth as the sea of the Lord, and flow like the "waters of Shiloah" to the sea of nations (see Isa. 8:6). They "possess the sea and the south." The sea was the western boundary of Palestine; therefore in Hebrew the west is called the sea. The spread of the gospel has always been rather to the west than to the east. To interpret Moses' prophecy of the geographical position of Naphtali is difficult. Some have understood it as a prophetic injunction to possess the Sea of Galilee to the south end. But as everything else which is said of Naphtali has a spiritual aspect, so probably this clause should be taken to agree with the rest. Not only to the far west shall the gospel extend the inheritance of its messengers, but to the south also. The north in Hebrew is the "hidden" region; the south is the land "enlightened" by the sun. May not the words of Moses have been partly fulfilled when Naphtali possessed the land enlightened by Jesus Christ? May they speedily be verified by the extension of the gospel as far as west and south can be measured, as far as the feet of God's messengers can go!

The great battle of Naphtali, in the days of the judges (Judg. 4), prefigured well the conflict of the apostles and evangelists in later times. Out of Kedesh-Naphtali, the very heart and center of Galilee, came Barak, the saviour of Israel, with ten thousand of Naphtali and Zebulun, to release his country from the oppressor's yoke. "Zebulun was a people that exposed his soul to reproach even unto death, and Naphtali on the high places of the field" (5:18). Even thus did "God

set forth the apostles last, as it were appointed unto death, a specta-
cle to the world, and to angels, and to men;" and they wrestled
against "spiritual wickedness" (Eph. 6:12) in the places of the field.
If the song of Deborah and Barak was prophetic of this greater conflict, we can better understand the remarkable force of its language,
and the strong feeling that it implies.

The men of Naphtali seem to have been always remarkable as
warriors. In the hands of the 37,000 who came to David at Hebron (1
Chron. 12:34), we find a weapon not named elsewhere in that
description of the soldiers of the tribes. The spear that was so formi-
dable in the hands of Saul and of Goliath was the weapon of
Naphtali, and no doubt they used it with effect. But the tribe of
Naphtali was one of the first that went into captivity, the first to feel
the destroying hand of Syrian and Assyrian kings. When the Lord
begins to cut Israel short, her evangelists are sure to fall.

If Tishbite means a man of Thisbe, in the tribe of Naphtali, as is
commonly supposed, Elijah the Tishbite (see 1 Ki. 17), the great
restorer of Israel, the typical forerunner of the Lord in all ages, is a
worthy representative of this tribe. That the great evangelist of the
Old Testament Scripture should be a man of Naphtali is only what we
should expect.

We may notice, also, that when all the tribes marched in the
wilderness, and all their rulers brought offerings at the dedication of
the altar, Naphtali's place and offering were the last (Num. 7:78). It
must be so with the preachers of the gospel. Their work continues to
the end. As long as the Day of Grace is still unexpired, even by a
moment, there is work for Naphtali to do in preaching the gospel to
sinners, to compel them to come in, to bring them as an offering to
the Lord. The last that are brought near to Jehovah are among the followers of Naphtali, the offering that he brings to the Lord. Thus we
may call Naphtali the missionary tribe.

Another feature that we have not noticed is common to the missionary character. Naphtali was parted from Dan his brother, found a
companion for his work here in Zebulun, and in Manasseh for his life
hereafter among the sealed of the living God. Nothing makes men so

solitary at first, or so certainly sets them in families afterwards, as the work of preaching the gospel of Christ. They leave house and brethren for His service; they receive "manifold more in this life present" (Lev. 18:30); and an everlasting recompense in the world to come. So Naphtali lost his brother Dan in Israel upon earth. Manasseh was divided through following Joshua, who brought him out of the inheritance of Moses into a better land. The two halves are again united, and the bereaved and the divided tribe are found together in the sealed of the thousands of Israel before the throne.[1]

1. See "The Order of the Sealed Tribes," a later study in this book, pp. 125-133.

10
GAD

Gad, a troop shall overcome him: but he shall overcome at the last.
GENESIS 49:19

And of Gad he said, Blessed be he that enlargeth Gad:
he dwelleth as a lion, and teareth the arm with the crown of the
head. And he provided the first part for himself, because there,
in a portion of the law giver, was he seated; and he came with the
heads of the people, he executed the justice of the Lord,
and his judgments with Israel.
Deuteronomy 33:20-21

No name in all the twelve tribes of Israel is so much played upon
in Jacob's blessing as the name of Gad. It signifies a troop, according to the use of the word in the Old Testament; and this word, or at
least the chief syllable of it, comes four times over in this verse in the
forty-ninth chapter of Genesis. It is somewhat as if we had read,
"This troop, a troop shall troop over him; but he shall troop at the
last." And it is not so easy to see what sort of a troop is meant.
However, in the greater number of passages where the troop is mentioned under this name, it means a troop of invaders, robbers, and

spoilers. The band of the Amalekites who burnt David's town of Ziklag (see 1 Sam. 30:1-6) is called by the name used in this verse, a company of plunderers, who made an invasion into the country to do all the harm they could. In other parts of the history of Israel we often read of such bands—bands of Syrians, bands of Moabites, bands of Chaldeans, bands of the children of Amnon. We should think them little better than bands of robbers, and so they often were.

But what was Leah thinking when she gave such a name to her adopted son (Gen. 30:11)? A strange thing, to connect him by name with a band of robbers! Perhaps she thought of her rivalry with her sister Rachel. Dan and Naphtali, who were born before, were counted as Rachel's children. Here was Gad, as it were a troop for Leah, to carry off some of the honor and glory for her. Or it may be that her thoughts were higher, and that she did not forget the glory of the God of Israel in the work that these children might hereafter do.

However, the picture before us in the name of Gad is a band of rovers going forth to win what they may—a strange picture if it is to be applied to the history of the Church of God and the followers of the Lord Jesus. And yet there may be something for our instruction here yet. In the list of the thousands of Israel in Revelation, only Judah, who prevailed above his brethren, and Reuben the firstborn, are before this tribe of Gad (Rev. 7:5). The words of Moses' blessing also indicate that he had a high opinion of the position and capabilities of the tribe. But he must first be overcome. "Gad, a troop shall overcome him, but he shall overcome at the last" (Gen. 49:19).

Many a good soldier of Jesus Christ has proved the truth of this. He was going to make such havoc among the hosts of God's enemies—to do such great things for Him, and gain such glory—and lo! before he had done anything, he was himself invaded and trampled to the ground, and almost crushed by the enemies of his own soul. The disciple who drew the sword and struck for his Master, when the band of men came with Judas (Jn. 18:10), denied his Master for fear of a woman before the night was gone (v. 17). And yet he did overcome at the last, and was crucified, going without his Master—and yet with Him—to prison and to death.

84

This is the history of many soldiers of Jesus Christ. The command given to them is to "endure hardness" (2 Tim. 2:3). What is it to endure hardness? To suffer ill treatment from the enemy, to endure afflictions, temptations, persecutions, just as in battle the soldier must sometimes be under the fire of the enemy and receive many attacks before he can be allowed to make the attack himself.

"Know ye that Ramoth in Gilead is ours, and we be still, and take it not out of the hand of the king of Syria?" (1 Ki. 22:3). So said the king of Israel to the king of Judah on a certain well-known occasion. It was of the chief Levitical city in the tribe of Gad that he spoke. The contest for this city of Ramoth Gilead, which was the rightful inheritance of the Gadites, lasted out the reigns of three kings of Israel. It was the death of one of them, and very nearly the death of two. That is an illustration of the case. They did recover that city at last, but not till they had been well beaten in the attempt; and after all, it was by the word of the Lord through His prophets.

Elisha, on his death-bed, foretold three victories over Syria for king Joash (2 Ki. 13:14-19); and Jonah foretold the victories of Jeroboam, who restored the coast of Israel from north to south, and took the Syrian capital itself (see 2 Ki. 14:25). They must, therefore, have recovered Ramoth Gilead, but not when they said "a troop cometh," and thought to take it out of hand. This is an illustration of the prophecy, "Gad, a troop shall overcome him, but he shall overcome at the last."

The land which fell to Gad's inheritance was peculiarly exposed to roving bands of marauders from the East. For the same reason, the country is notoriously unsafe for travelers at the present day. It was chosen by the Gadites, with the Reubenites and half the tribe of Manasseh, because there was good pasture in Gilead for their flocks. They desired it in spite of all dangers. Moses at first checked their desire, and then consented to it when he understood. But evidently the Gadites were the leaders in that enterprise, and Moses treated them so in the blessing which he gave. In Numbers 32:1, the historian says, the children of Reuben and Gad had cattle, naming Reuben the eldest first; but when he comes to the account of their position to

Moses, it is not Reuben but Gad who takes the lead (v. 2): "The children of Gad and the children of Reuben came and spake unto Moses, and to Eleazar." So it is wherever their names are mentioned in the rest of the chapter (vv. 25, 29, 31, 33).

Their inheritance was given to them on the east of Jordan in the mountains of Gilead on one condition. They must go over armed, or, at least, the main body of them, with Joshua, before the rest of the tribes, to win the land for their brethren; and, when the conquest was completed, they might go back and enjoy their own. It is to this that the blessing given them by Moses partly refers. Gad is one of the three tribes that are likened to lions among the twelve. And of Gad he said, "Blessed be he that enlargeth Gad," (i.e., makes room for him). His position was closely hemmed in on all sides. He was between the Jordan and the mountains—Reuben on one side of him to the south, Manasseh to the north, the Ammonites on the east pressing him in, and the Moabites not far off.

The men who would choose such a position must be prepared to run the risk of invasion. Their flocks and herds would be a perpetual temptation to their neighbors, and they must learn to hold their own. But there they chose to dwell, like the lions by the banks of Jordan, in the thickets and on the mountain slopes. Moses blessed those that should make room for them. "He dwelleth as a lion," and like a lion he "teareth the arm with the crown of the head;" and "he provided the first part for himself, because there the portion of the lawgiver" (i.e., a portion given by Moses) was preserved.[1] He was hidden and protected there by the covert of the mountains on the east, and the river on the west—a very strong position if it could only be retained.

There is some important lesson intended in the fact that the tribes on the east of Jordan received their inheritance from Moses, and not

1. Some render it, "there the sepulcher of the lawgiver was concealed." I cannot decide the critical questions involved in the interpretation of the clause, but I think the idea is that Gad himself, in the inheritance of the lawgiver, found a safe retreat. Some think that the thing preserved was the inheritance itself, and the words will perhaps bear this meaning.

from Joshua, and yet were compelled to attend Joshua in his warfare before they could go back to the inheritance that Moses had given them first. It reminds us of the distinction drawn in Hebrews 11, between the Old Testament saints and ourselves: "These all, having obtained a good report through faith, received not the promise; God having provided some better thing for us, that they without us should not be made perfect" (vv. 39-40). And yet the believers of the Old Testament and of the New are linked together there, just as the Gadites and the army of Joshua are; for Moses continues concerning Gad, "He came with the heads of the people, and executed the justice of the Lord and His judgments with Israel."

This will refer first of all, prophetically, to the conquest of Canaan, when the warriors of the tribe of Gad went over before their brethren, and executed the justice of the Lord on the seven nations whom He destroyed before them (Josh. 4:12). And after that there is very probably a reference to the time of David, when a most remarkable thing is recorded of the tribe.

In the list of those who came to David in the wilderness, when he was still a fugitive in the days of Saul, we read thus: "And of the Gadites there separated themselves unto David into the hold to the wilderness men of might, and men of war, fit for the battle, that could handle shield and buckler, whose faces were like the faces of lions, and were as swift as the roes upon the mountains." (Here follow eleven names.) "These are they that went over Jordan in the first month, when it had overflown all it's banks; and they put to flight all them of the valleys, both of the east and of the west" (see 1 Chron. 12:8, 15).

Here is the lion-like character of Gad still retained with even greater strength and vigor than before. The Gadites who crossed the Jordan with Joshua crossed in the first month also, and Jordan "overflows all his banks all the time of harvest" (Josh. 3:15), but Joshua's army went over dry-shod, for the Lord divided it before them. It seems that the eleven Gadites of the time of David swam the river when it was at its full height, in order to be with him. Their names were all recorded, and they are full of significance (1 Chron. 12:9-

13). Seven of the names contain part of the name Jehovah, or the name of God. These also, as helpers of David, "executed the justice of the Lord, and His judgments with Israel." "The noble army of martyrs praise Thee."[2]

It would seem that the experience of Gad, and the trials of his inheritance, afforded a training profitable, and sometimes necessary, for other members of the family of Israel. This land afforded a place of refuge from enemies on the west. In the Philistine invasion in the reign of Saul, we read that "some of the Hebrews went over Jordan to the land of Gad and Gilead" (1 Sam. 13:7). If these Hebrews thought that by going over to Gad's inheritance they would escape the necessity of fighting for the land that God had given them, they probably found themselves in the wrong; for in the days of Saul occurred the great war against the Hagarites, by which the eastern tribes extended their inheritance from Jordan to the river Euphrates (1 Chron. 5:10-11). This war was undertaken in the spirit of faith, for we read, "They cried to God in the battle, and he was entreated of them, because they put their trust in Him" (v. 20).

Thus did Gad overcome the bands of those that spoiled him—fulfilling the prophecy of Jacob, that he should "overcome at the last." But there is one personage in Old Testament history who was also compelled to take refuge in the land of Gilead—we are not told why, but it is not hard to guess. "Elijah the Tishbite, who was of the inhabitants of Gilead" (1 Ki. 17:1), may well have been a man like one of those eleven Gadites, with a face as the face of a lion, and as light of foot as a wild roe. Remember how he ran before Ahab from Carmel to the entrance of Jezreel (1 Ki. 18:46).

It is not a little interesting to see how it is made out that Elijah was

2. The help afforded by the two-and-a-half tribes to their brethren may well represent the help given to the followers of the true Joshua in all ages by their brethren who found rest in the inheritance given them by Moses long before. All the blessings which we derive from the history and experience of Old Testament saints come under this head. Those who think of the two-and-a-half tribes as mere "borderers" have only half the truth.

sent to Gilead from his home. We find it in the first words that are said of him in 1 Kings 17. "Elijah the Tishbite, who was of the inhabitants of Gilead," is what we read. Tishbite is commonly explained to mean a native of Thisbe, a town on the right hand of Kedesh-Naphtali, mentioned in the apocryphal book of Tobit (1:2). But the Hebrew word for inhabitant, in every other place where it occurs in the Old Testament, is rendered stranger or sojourner, and so it ought to be here: "Elijah, the Tishbite (of Thisbe, by Kedesh-Naphtali), who was of the sojourners in Gilead, spake to Ahab…"

What an interesting fact in Elijah's early history is thus revealed! He, like many a good man before him, had been compelled to go over Jordan to the land of Gad, probably to escape the persecution of Jezebel, who "cut off the prophets of the Lord" (1 Ki. 18:4). There, among the mountains of Gilead, he was prepared for the work of his ministry. There, in a new sense, "the portion of the lawgiver Moses was preserved." Alone with God in the desert, like Moses in the wilderness of Sinai, like Paul in Arabia, Elijah learned what God would have him do. But, by taking refuge in Gilead, Elijah the Tishbite of Naphtali (the great missionary tribe) became a Gadite also, and learned the ways of the mighty men of that tribe. A man of Naphtali sojourning in Gilead, he learned to make the Lord God of Israel his inheritance, to do His bidding, and to lean on no one but Him.

And it was from the land of Gilead that Elijah was taken up in the chariot of fire. There Moses had passed away before Elijah crossed the Jordan with Elisha, on that last day of his pilgrimage, near Jericho, and from there went up to heaven. In him above all others we seem to see the fulfillment of Jacob's prophecy, "Gad, a troop shall overcome him, but he shall overcome at the last." Perhaps no man of God was ever so hard pressed by the bands of his enemies as Elijah. No one ever gained a more complete victory in the end. Not only in his ascension, in the successor that he left behind him, and in his appearance with Moses on that Holy Mount, to see the glory of the Saviour and talk with Him, but in this also he overcame—in that his name is inseparably connected with the reformation of God's people, and the restoration of true religion, to the end of the world. "Elias truly shall first come and restore all things" (Mt. 17:11). "The spirit and power of Elijah" (Lk. 1:17) is the Bible name for the spirit of true reformation until the Day of the Lord.

And the land of Gad and Gilead is especially consecrated by the sojourning of Elijah and the preaching of John the Baptist, who was in that region when he gave his testimony to Jesus as the Lamb of God. There, again and again, the portion of the lawgiver was preserved. Thence came Elijah to the king and the heads of the people, "and executed the justice of the Lord, and His judgments with Israel."

God's children sometimes learn more in solitary conflict, when they feel utterly overcome by their enemies, than in the times of prosperity and peace. At least we may be sure that all God's servants, who are to do great things for Him, must go and sojourn in the land of Gad and Gilead first. There is Jordan to be crossed, and there might be heard in ancient times the roar of the lions driven up from the thickets by the flood. "He shall come up like a lion from the swelling of Jordan" (Jer. 49:19). There are to be met the swift-footed warriors of the Gadites, with whom we may fairly ask ourselves, "If thou hast run with the footmen, and they have wearied thee, then how canst thou contend with horses? and if in the land of peace, wherein thou trustest, they wearied thee, then how wilt thou do in the swelling of Jordan?" (Jer. 12:5). "If thou faint in the day of adversity, thy strength is small" (Prov. 24:10). And there is the balm of Gilead to be gathered, and to know the Physician that is there, that the health of the daughter of Israel may be recovered in due time (see Jer. 8:22).

These things, and the significance of them, may be learned by sojourners in the land of the Gadites, but will scarcely be learned elsewhere. And no one who does not understand some of the meaning of these conflicts is ever likely to accomplish a great work for God. No one, who has not felt himself overcome by tough bands of the enemy, is likely to bring a band of followers into the golden city, or to "overcome at the last." But "he that goeth forth and weepeth, bearing precious seed, shall doubtless come again with rejoicing, bringing his sheaves with him" (Ps. 126:6).

11
ASHER

Out of Asher his bread shall be fat,
and he shall yield royal dainties.
Genesis 49:20

And of Asher he said, Let Asher be blessed with children;
let him be acceptable to his brethren, and let him dip his foot in oil.
Thy shoes shall be iron and brass; and as thy days,
so shall thy strength be.
Deuteronomy 33:24-25

Of all the tribes of Israel, the tribe of Asher has the least eventful history. There is no great warrior, no judge, no king, no counselor of Asher conspicuous in the people of God. The very land of Asher is as uneventful as the tribe itself. No great battles were fought there in the time of Israel's history, so far as we can tell. No places in that inheritance come into notice. This is all the more remarkable when we see how very famous one place which was given to the tribe of Asher has since become. The port and the town of Acre have been fought again and again, and regarded as nothing less than the key of Palestine. It was on the shore of that bay surrounding that town that the men of Asher dwelt so peaceably. In this view their quietness is no credit to them. In the book of Judges it is mentioned as a fault that they left the important places which God gave them in the hands of the former inhabitants of the land (Judg. 1:31-32). "Neither did Asher drive out the inhabitants of Accho," since called Acre, "nor the inhabitants of Sidon." Accho and Sidon were two of the important places that Asher might have had. Even in the great battle with the Canaanites, when Jabin and Sisera were overthrown by Barak's army, "Asher continued on the seashore, and abode in the creeks" (5:17).

In the time of David, there were forty thousand of Asher that went forth to battle, expert in war, who came to David to Hebron, with the rest of the people, to make him king (1 Chron. 12:36-38). But, with one exception,[1] we have no record that the tribe of Asher rendered assistance in the wars of Israel.

The blessings of Jacob and Moses imply that Asher would have a rich and fertile country, and so it came to pass. "Out of Asher," Jacob said, "his bread shall be fat, and he shall yield royal dainties." And Moses adds, "Let Asher be acceptable to his brethren." Those who dwell in the midst of plenty, and are willing to share it, always are most acceptable to their brethren! "And let him dip his foot in oil." One whose dwelling was the fatness of the earth might very properly be said to dip his foot in oil. This may be an allusion to the olive trees, for that part of Palestine is said to have been thickly wooded— a land of corn and wine and oil—with fertile plains and valleys defended by the mountains. And if the supplies of the country failed the inhabitants, their ports enabled them to bring in provisions from the sea. It may have been of some importance to Israel that a peaceable tribe like Asher should occupy this part of the land, for the territory of Asher adjoined that of the Phoenicians, who might have been troublesome enemies, but were generally well disposed.

In the time of David and Solomon, the kings of Tyre and Israel were friends. The timber for the building of the Temple was brought

1. The tribe of Asher joined Gideon in his pursuit of the Midianite (Judg. 6:35; 7:23).

from Lebanon, by the consent of the Phoenician kings (2 Sam. 5:11; 1 Ki. 5:1, 10-12). One would think that the influence of the northern tribe of Asher must have had something to do with this friendship; but, at any rate, the people of Tyre and Sidon were brought into some kind of connection with the God of Israel, and had some knowledge of Him. Two of the Psalms seem to hint at this. "And the daughter of Tyre shall be there with a gift" (45:12); and "I will make mention of Rahab and Babylon to them that know Me. Behold Philistia, and Tyre, with Ethiopia: this man was born there" (87:4).

Only once is there a hint of enmity (Ps. 83:6-7). And though in the time of Ahab, who took to wife a daughter of the king of the Sidonians (1 Ki. 16:31), the connection between the Phoenicians and Israel was too close and became disastrous, yet, upon the whole, perhaps more good than evil arose out of the fact that there was peace between the tribe of Asher and his neighbors to the north.

Thus far, we have looked only at the outside history of the tribe, and the literal meaning of the prophecies that concern him; but this is neither the most interesting nor the most profitable part of the work; and we have now to inquire what kind of character and what sort of history are represented by the tribe of Asher, in those who are truly the people of God.

There is only one member of the tribe of whom enough is written in the Bible to give the sketch of a life; and that member is a widow, of whom we read in the New Testament. "There was one Anna, a prophetess, the daughter of Phanuel, of the tribe or Asher" (Lk. 2:36-38). This woman represents to us the individual history of the tribe. No other tribe is thus represented in Holy Scripture by a woman. What makes it still more peculiar is that no other of the ten tribes has any representative expressly named in the New Testament. Of course, all the tribes were in existence. Paul speaks of them; Peter and James wrote to them. Their continuance is implied in many passages. Our Saviour dwelt on the borders of Zebulun and Naphtali; His apostles, for the most part, probably belonged to those two tribes; but there is no other person in the New Testament who is expressly said to be of any one of the ten tribes that formed the house of Joseph and the separate kingdom of Israel. Benjamin and Judah and Levi have many representatives in the New Testament; but the ten tribes of Israel have only "Anna…a widow of the tribe of Asher," to represent them all. It is another instance of God's choosing the weak things of the world to confound the strong.

One aged man, Simeon, on the part of Judah, confessed the Saviour of the world when he was brought as an infant into the Temple, and took Him up in his arms (vv. 25-35); and Anna confessed Him on the part of Israel—a widow woman of the tribe of Asher, the least honored and least conspicuous of all the twelve tribes. This fact necessarily gives a feminine aspect to the character of Asher in the Word of God; and certainly the things commended in Asher by Jacob and Moses are virtues that more generally become the daughters of Israel than the men. The studying to be quiet, not coming forward into public life or taking the lead, but keeping peace on the borders and abiding at home—all this is very much the kind of life that is recommended in the epistles for Christian women. To "give none occasion to the adversary to speak reproachfully, to be discreet, to be keepers at home, to have the ornament of a meek and quiet spirit, which is in the sight of God of great price"—these are some of the precepts of the two leading apostles on the subject (see Titus 2:5; 1 Pet. 3:4).

Let us now inquire for the marks of redemption in the history of this character. None can enter any of the twelve gates of Israel's city who have not washed their robes and made them white in the blood of the Lamb (see Rev. 7:14). And from what particular sin are the Israelites of the tribe of Asher to be redeemed? What is the defect of the natural character? What is the chief excellence of the renewed character, when it is "washed, and sanctified, and justified, in the name of the Lord Jesus and by the Spirit of our God" (1 Cor. 6:11)?

The chief defect in the character of Asher is the love of ease. The people of this tribe could not drive out the Canaanites, but dwelt among them. It is said of other tribes that the Canaanites dwelt among them, and would dwell among them. But it is said that Asher dwelt among the Canaanites (Judg. 1:32), not attempting to take exclusive possession of the land, but settling down quietly wherever there was room, content if only it was possible to dwell in peace.

Of course this was the easier plan; but it was not the way commanded to Israel by Moses or Joshua, according to the law of the Lord. The command was that they should utterly drive out the nations, and make no terms with them. Disobedience to that commandment brought many troubles on the people of God. Yet Asher persisted in this course, refusing even to help against the great army of the Canaanites, when the neighboring tribes were exposing their lives "unto the death in the high places of the field" (Judg. 5:18). Only when the corn and the wine and the oil were consumed by the Midianites could Asher be induced to join in the battle. This is love of ease and peace carried to an excess, and it can only be condemned.

But now look at the other side of the picture. This character may become very lovely, when, instead of resting in earthly happiness, it consents to rest in the Lord. That is the turning-point. There is one thing recorded of Asher in the Old Testament that illustrates it. About the time of the captivity of the ten tribes of Israel, Hezekiah sent messengers throughout the whole country to invite the people to come up to Jerusalem to keep the passover unto the Lord (2 Chron. 30:1). This was an attempt at reformation, for "they had not done it of a long time, in such sort as it was written" (v. 5).

The messengers were mocked and laughed to scorn. But there were some who acted differently; and of these Asher was the first. "Divers of Asher and Manasseh and Zebulun, humbled themselves and came to Jerusalem" (2 Chron. 30:11). Asher, that was most willing to rest in his own inheritance, was also the first to humble himself, and come to "rest in the Lord" (see Ps. 37:7).

The next mention of the tribe in history is in the second chapter of Luke. This tribe was most willing to come to Jerusalem in the days of Hezekiah; it abides in the same place in the New Testament. There Asher is found represented in the person of Anna, who had come to dwell at Jerusalem, to attend the House of the Lord continually, and no more depart. No longer dwelling among the Canaanites, or abiding safely in the creeks by the seashore, nor even finding rest as a bride in the house of her husband; but carrying out the spirit of what is said by David, "How lovely are Thy dwellings, O Lord of hosts. My soul longeth, yea; even fainteth for the courts of the Lord; my heart and my flesh crieth out for the living God. Yea, the sparrow hath found her an house"—the lonely one that sat on the house-top has found a home, even within Thy house, and within Thy walls—"even Thine altars, O Lord of hosts, my King and my God" (Ps. 84:1-3).

Whether for those that are solitary, like the widowed Anna, or for those that are set in families, there is one resting place; and it is to rest in the Lord. And see what followed in the story of Anna. The tribe that had never spoken or fought for Israel before, found a voice in her. She that had departed from her own home in Asher, but departed not from the Temple, found something to say for Israel, and for the glory of God. She became a prophetess in her widowhood, and never did she find a better subject for prophecy than on the day when she came into the Temple, and found Mary and Joseph and the Saviour of the world. Then she, like Simeon before her, "gave thanks unto the Lord, and spake of Him to all them that looked for redemption in Jerusalem" (Lk. 2:38).

We may now return to the prophecies concerning Asher in the books of Moses, and read their spiritual meaning by the light of the facts that we have seen. Enough has been said already of their literal fulfillment. Asher was the second son of Zilpah, the handmaid of Leah. Some of Leah's other children, in the names that she gave them, carried the memorials of her alienation, her struggles to obtain the favor of her husband, and satisfy her desires. In the birth of Asher she confessed herself satisfied (Gen. 30:13). She said, "In my happiness, for the daughters will call me blessed: and she called his name Asher," i.e., happy.

We have seen how this character remained with the tribe throughout. There was at first happiness obtained by resting in a rich and fertile part of Canaan, and at last a happiness still better, obtained by rejoicing in the Lord. We have seen the prophecies applied to the earthly happiness. Let us see whether they may not also be taken of the spiritual portion.

Jacob said of his son Asher, (i) that out of Asher his bread should be fat; and (ii) he shall give royal dainties. Here is, first, the happiness of enjoying; secondly, the still greater happiness of giving. "Out of Asher"—i.e., from his inheritance—"his bread shall be fat." This may be the bread that comes down from heaven, as well as perishable food. "In this mountain" (i.e., the mountain of the House of the Lord, the last resting-place of Asher, when the tribe was humbled) "in this mountain shall the Lord of hosts make unto all people a feast of fat things" (Isa. 25:6). The oil of gladness is there. A daily anointing with fresh oil may be obtained from the Holy Spirit that fell on the hill of Zion—the true dew of heaven that calls forth the fatness of the earth. There it may be said by those who come continually to feed on the bread of heaven, "Surely goodness and mercy shall follow me all the days of my life, and I will dwell in the house of the Lord forever" (Ps. 23:6).

The true meaning of the inheritance of Asher is to keep the Saviour's command, "Abide in Me." The fatness of the bread of Asher is the anointing received of the Holy One, of which John says to the disciples, "It abideth in you, and even as it hath taught you, ye shall abide in Him" (1 Jn. 2:27). There is no way for the soul to dwell at ease except this; it must stop seeking rest in the things of earth, and humble itself to go up to Jerusalem, and seek rest in things above.

But when the inheritance has been obtained from the Lord Jesus, as the tribe of Asher received its portion at the hand of Joshua, then out of the abundance of the heart the lips will speak. "His bread shall be fat," and he shall give to others—"give royal dainties." He will speak of the pleasures that are at the right hand of the King. Thus did the prophetess who rejoiced in the Saviour herself, and had rejoiced in His Temple for so many years, speak of Him to all them that looked for redemption in Jerusalem.

Thus Jacob's blessing of Asher becomes a prophecy of rejoicing in Christ, and of work for Christ. Moses takes it up at the point where Jacob leaves it. "Let Asher be blessed with children," literally blessed from sons. When Asher was born, Leah said, "The daughters will call me blessed" (Gen. 30:13). Moses said, "Let him be blessed from sons," i.e., blessed either from the multitude of his sons, or because his sons should call him blessed. A large family of sons in Asher's genealogy in Chronicles illustrates this. But I think it has a spiritual meaning. Those who bring forth the royal dainties received at the King's table, and then set them before others, shall be blessed with spiritual children, blessed by the voices of those to whom they minister. That this may be the portion of Asher is Moses' prayer. For he continues, "Let him be acceptable to his brethren, and let him[2] dip his foot in oil." There could not be a more suitable prayer for those who are to speak to their brethren of the things of God. May God make them acceptable in what they say.

The dipping of the foot in oil suggests several things. The priest that was consecrated in Israel, and the leper that was cleansed of his leprosy, and once more admitted into the congregation, must both alike be touched with blood and with oil upon the ear, and upon the hand and the foot (Ex. 29:20; Lev. 14). As Christ said, "He that is washed, needeth not save to wash his feet" (Jn. 13:10), so it might be said, "He that is anointed, and has the anointing from the Holy One, needeth not save to anoint his foot daily, that the preparation of the gospel of peace may ever be fresh upon him, that he may be always ready to minister and speak to his brethren as the oracles of God."

The words that complete the blessing are a wonderful promise of endurance for the days of the pilgrimage to the end. "Thy shoes shall be iron and brass, and as thy days, so shall thy strength be." The word for shoes, and the word for strength, are both peculiar to this verse, and found nowhere else in the Bible, and various conjectures have been made as to the true meaning. But the interpretation given in our English Bible is the oldest, older than the New Testament, and there seems no reason to doubt that it is right. Such a promise would be well understood, by those whom the Lord had led through the great and terrible wilderness, whose "raiment waxed not old upon them, neither did their foot swell" for forty years (see Deut. 8:4). It is well illustrated in the story of Anna, who was long past eighty when she

2. Literally, "Let him be one that dippeth (continually) his foot in oil."

98

saw the Saviour, and spoke of Him to all that looked for redemption in Jerusalem.

Even so, "the righteous shall flourish as a palm tree, he shall grow as a cedar in Lebanon. Those that be planted in the house of the Lord shall flourish in the courts of our God. They shall still bring forth fruit in old age; they shall be fat and flourishing. To show that the Lord is upright: He is my rock, and there is no unrighteousness in Him" (Ps. 92:12-15).

12
MANASSEH

And unto Joseph were born two sons before the years of famine
came, which Asenath the daughter of Potipherah priest of On bare
unto him. And Joseph called the name of the firstborn Manasseh:
For God, said he, hath made me forget all my toil,
and all my father's house.
GENESIS 41:50-51

And his father refused, and said, I know it, my son, I know it:
he also shall become a people, and he also shall be great:
but truly his younger brother shall be greater than he,
and his seed shall become a multitude of nations.
GENESIS 48:19

His glory is like the firstling of his bullock, and his horns are like
the horns of unicorns: with them he shall push the people together
to the ends of the earth: and they are the ten thousands of Ephraim,
and they are the thousands of Manasseh.
DEUTERONOMY 33:17

"Manasseh shall be a people, and he shall be great," is the portion given by Jacob to this tribe. Moses speaks of the thousands of Manasseh side by side with the ten thousands of his brother Ephraim; but there is more character about the name of Manasseh than appears in those two fragments of prophecy which can be limited to him.

The first thing to remark is, that Ephraim and Manasseh may fairly be called Jacob's Gentile descendants. They were children of an Egyptian mother, born while their father Joseph occupied the position of a Gentile prince. Accordingly, when we remember the words respecting Ephraim, that his seed should be "the fullness[1] of the Gentiles," we can only regard Joseph as representing Christ, the Saviour of the Gentile world. The tribe of Judah is sacred to our Lord as head of the chosen people. The character of Joseph belongs to Him[2] in prophecy as the Saviour of all mankind; and as in the twelve tribes we find the house of Judah and the house of Joseph united, so in the Church of Christ—the Bride, the Lamb's Wife—we find the gate of Joseph open for the Gentiles in multitudes that no man can number.

But this subject belongs rather to Ephraim. Manasseh stands nearer to the Jews, and seems to be a kind of link between the Gentile and the Jew. In his birth we see Joseph looking two ways, "forgetting," and yet mentioning, "all his toil, and all his father's house" (Gen. 41:51). Manasseh's inheritance in the land of Canaan occupies the same kind of place. This tribe alone was divided by express permission into two halves. One half of Manasseh took its inheritance from Moses, on the eastern side of Jordan; the other half received a portion from Joshua, on the western side. The whole tribe went over to

1. Gen. 48:19. Multitude of nations; literally, the fullness of the Gentiles.

2. If it is thought necessary to prove that Joseph is a type of Christ (a fact which every child accepts without reasoning), it may be observed that Christ Himself implied it by applying to Himself words originally spoken of Joseph, "Come, let us kill him." See the Greek of Mt. 21:38; Gen. 37:20 (Sept.). The name Joseph (Jehoseph in Ps. 81:5) is the first in Scripture which clearly contains a part of the name Jehovah.

fight the battles of Israel against the seven nations; but when it came to settle in its inheritance, there was a part that went back as well as a part that went forward, and the river Jordan was the barrier between.

During the forty years' march in the wilderness, the tribe of Manasseh increased greatly. Ephraim, on the contrary, was diminished in the number of its fighting men. The whole of Ephraim only exceeded the half of Manasseh, when the tribe was divided, by some 6,000 men (Num. 26:34-37). The men of Manasseh who received their inheritance from Moses were favored in this respect; for they were the possessors of that wonderful volcanic region of Argob, the kingdom of Og, in Bashan, with its threescore cities, and their high walls, gates, and bars—the giant cities of Bashan, gigantic in their desolation even to this day. There was no stronger position than Argob in all Israel's land.

The tribe of Manasseh in the history of the Judges produced two out of the four men whose faith has been thought worthy of notice in the New Testament—Gideon and Jephthah. Perhaps it enhances the value of Jephthah's loss for the sake of Israel to remember the law of inheritance, so especially laid down for the sake of the tribe of Manasseh (see Num. 27; 36), by which law the daughter of Jephthah might have perpetuated the name of her father, but for his vow (Judg. 11:30-40).

The two stories of Gideon and Jephthah supply the only recorded instances of jealousy between Manasseh and Ephraim, the two brother tribes. How jealous Ephraim was for his position, the complaint of the Ephraimites against the judges of Manasseh will clearly show. "They did chide with Gideon sharply," because they said he had not called them to go with him, and he gave them a soft answer (8:1ff).

Not so Jephthah, who answered them in kind, and gathered all the men of Gilead together and smote them, because they called the Gileadites "fugitives of Ephraim" (12:4). It was the men of Manasseh who first imposed the famous test of "Shibboleth" upon those of Ephraim, that they might discover who their enemies were (v. 6). That test of "Shibboleth" cost the Ephraimites 42,000 men!

The popular application of that story, as we shall see, is curiously near the truth.

Jair the Gileadite, Jephthah's predecessor, was also probably of Manasseh, and his history recalls another interesting incident that throws light on the law of inheritance. By his grandfather's side, Jair[3] was a man of Judah, his grandmother was of Manasseh, and the family inheritance remained in the latter tribe (1 Chron. 2:21-23).

There is nothing after this in the history of the tribe that seems to call for special mention until we come to the captivity of the kingdom of Israel, and then we find frequent mention of Manasseh in the notices of the remnant of Israel that was left in the land. The captivity of the ten tribes of the kingdom of Israel took place in the reign of Hezekiah, king of Judah. After the captivity, he and his successors took notice of this remnant, and endeavored to draw all the Israelites together into one kingdom, at least for religious purposes, and in several instances with success (2 Chron. 30). We find that a multitude of Ephraim and Manasseh, Issachar and Zebulun, came up to the Passover in Hezekiah's reign, and that in Josiah's reign the Levites collected money from Ephraim and Manasseh, and all the remnant of Israel, to repair the temple at Jerusalem (2 Chron. 34:9). Also, by 1 Chronicles 9:3, it appears that some of Ephraim and Manasseh returned from the Babylonish captivity with Judah and Benjamin in the reign of Cyrus, and dwelt at Jerusalem. There was therefore probably a remnant of these tribes at Jerusalem in New Testament times.

If we may judge by the notices in the book of Revelation, the tribe of Manasseh preserves its separate existence somewhat more than the tribe of Ephraim. The name of Ephraim is not among the list of those who were sealed of the children of Israel, but gives place to Joseph, and the name of Joseph is probably on the gate of pearl. Neither Manasseh nor Ephraim have gates in the city described in Ezekiel 48. There is one gate of Joseph for the two; so that Ephraim is not mentioned by name in the New Testament, while we find that

3. Or possibly an ancestor of the same name.

"of the tribe of Manasseh were sealed 12,000" (Rev. 7:6).

Thus far we have the history of the tribe. And now what may that history mean? If we are right in supposing that Joseph represents Christ as the Saviour of the Gentiles, and Manasseh was the first son born to Joseph when he had just attained that position, it follows that we must look for one fulfillment of Manasseh's history in the earliest days of the Gentile Church. There I believe it may be found; and I think that this will suggest the meaning of the fact that Manasseh was divided into two halves. Both parts alike acknowledged the leadership of Joshua, and went over to the conquest of the seven nations. But when it came to the question on which side of Jordan they would have their own inheritance, one half of the tribe chose the portion of the lawgiver, and took what Moses had given them, while the others looked to Joshua alone.[4] Yet both were alike true Israelites.

Was not this exactly the position of many of the first believers in the Lord Jesus when His gospel was preached to the Gentiles? There were many Jews who preferred to keep the law of Moses still. "Thou seest, brother, how many thousands of Jews there are that believe (i.e., believe on Jesus), and they are all zealous of the law" (Acts 21:20). There were some, like Paul and his companions, who would mix freely with the Gentiles, looking for no privileges but such as Jew and Gentile received in common from the true Joshua, the Lord Jesus. Others, like Peter at Antioch, separated themselves and clung to Moses, still thinking that there was something better in the customs which they had inherited from him; and there were bitter jealousies in the early days of Christianity between these two parties.

And, just as the Manassites on the east of Jordan would make the Ephraimites of the western side say "Shibboleth" or die, so did the believers who continued to be followers of Moses persecute their brethren who were conformed to the true Joshua, and compel them to speak the language of the other side. What else was the advice

4. It is worthy of notice that the half tribe of Manasseh which remained with Joshua received a special blessing from him—the only recorded words of blessing that we have from Joshua's lips (Josh. 22:8).

105

given to Paul at Jerusalem by the brethren who favored the believers of that type, to go and purify himself as a Nazarite in the temple, but an attempt to make him say "Shibboleth" if he could? And what did he do in fact but say "Sibboleth"? for his attempt was only misunderstood. It succeeded so poorly that he was dragged out of the temple, and almost pulled to pieces by a savage mob.

The question, "Who began the quarrel?" is hardly worth asking. The difference between these two parties of believers was no more necessary than the quarrel between Manasseh and Ephraim, and yet probably in both cases there were faults on both sides.

Of the two brothers, Ephraim stands nearer to the Gentiles. The promise that hereafter there shall be one flock belongs especially to the union of the Gentile and the Jew (see Jn. 10:16, mar.). We sometimes forget that that was its first meaning, as it will be its last. The Good Shepherd has not left the lost sheep of the house of Judah when He said, "Other sheep I have which are not of this fold; them also I must bring, and there shall be one flock (not one fold, as we have it) and one Shepherd" (Jn. 10:16).

It has been sometimes found necessary, not only in ancient but in modern times, to choose between the portion of the lawgiver, and the inheritance that comes direct from Christ. Jealousies and disputes usually could have been avoided, yet in each case inevitably occur. There have been examples throughout church history, and there may be more to come.

Let us contrast the saying of Joseph at the birth of Manasseh with Jacob's blessing of the two sons of Joseph afterwards. When Manasseh was born, his father seemed to accept the separation from his own family as the final appointment of God. He ceased from simply longing after the home he had lost, accepted the work before him, and looked forward with confidence to the future. He called the name of his firstborn Manasseh, "one who forgets, for God hath caused me to forget all my toil, and all my father's house" (Gen. 41:51). How little did Joseph think that Manasseh would afterwards, in God's providence, become a most important member of that very house which his name seemed to forget! Not many years later, Jacob said, "God, before whom my fathers Abraham and Isaac did walk,…bless the lads; and let my name be named on them, and the name of my fathers, Abraham and Isaac, and let them grow into a multitude in the midst of the earth" (Gen. 48:15-16). Thus the very son, whose name seemed to perpetuate the separation of Joseph from the house of Jacob, was adopted by Jacob into his house afterwards, to be, as Reuben and Simeon, a head of one of the tribes of Israel to all eternity. Manasseh, the one who forgets his home in Israel on earth, is sealed forever in the "Israel of God."

Even so, "Many shall come from the east and west, and shall sit down with Abraham, Isaac, and Jacob in the kingdom of heaven" (Mt. 8:11); and of all that shall be so brought into God's house none shall have a richer portion than they who, for the sake of Christ and His gospel, were willing to forsake the labors and the profits of this life, and to suffer the loss of all things (or even of some things) that they might win Him. These are the sons born to the true Joseph in the land of His affliction, when His name is cast out as evil and His truth despised and rejected, His disciples persecuted, and His followers few. These are the spiritual children of Manasseh, but they have the spirit of adoption. God, the Shepherd of Israel, and "the Angel of the Covenant," His Redeemer, shall bless them. The name of the true Israel shall be named upon them, and "God is not ashamed to be called their God, for He hath prepared for them a city" (Heb. 11:16).

"Lo! we have left all and followed Thee; what shall we have therefore?" (Mt. 19:27). Joshua said to the half tribe of Manasseh that remained with him, "Return with much riches unto your tents, and with very much cattle, with silver, and with gold, and with brass, and with iron, and with very much raiment: divide the spoil of your enemies with your brethren" (Josh. 22:8). But Jesus answered and said, "Verily I say unto you, There is no man that hath left house, or brethren, or sisters, or father, or mother, or wife, or children, or lands, for My sake and the gospel's, but he shall receive an hundredfold now in this time, houses, and brethren, and sisters, and mothers, and children, and lands, with persecutions; and in the world to come eternal life" (Mk. 10:29-30).

13
EPHRAIM

And the name of the second called he Ephraim:
for God hath caused me to be fruitful in the land of my affliction.
GENESIS 41:52

And his father refused, and said, I know it, my son, I know it:
he also shall become a people, and he also shall be great:
but truly his younger brother shall be greater than he, and his seed
shall become a multitude of nations.
GENESIS 48:19

His glory is like the firstling of his bullock, and his horns are like
the horns of unicorns: with them he shall push the people together
to the ends of the earth: and they are the ten thousands of Ephraim,
and they are the thousands of Manasseh.
DEUTERONOMY 33:17

No tribe among all the children of Israel loses its individuality so
completely as the tribe of Ephraim. We have already noticed that
though there was a gate of Ephraim in Jerusalem on earth, there is no
gate of Ephraim in the city described in Ezekiel 48, and we must sup-

pose that Ephraim is not one of the names to be inscribed in the New Jerusalem upon a portico of pearl.

It is not recorded that of the tribe of Ephraim were sealed 12,000, though it may be that "the great multitude which no man can number, of all nations and kindreds, and people and tongues" (Rev. 7:9), are to be somehow reckoned to Ephraim in the world to come. I do not see how we can limit the prophecy that "His seed shall be the fullness of the Gentiles" (see Gen. 48:19; Num. 24:7), so as to identify him with any one nation of the Gentile world. The literal fulfillment of that prophecy can scarcely be explained by any theory that would connect Ephraim with ourselves. But the literal discovery of Ephraim, or any other individual tribe of Israel in modern times, is a question that I must leave.

It seems much easier to prove the analogy between the kingdom of Israel, which was always headed by Ephraim, and the Church. In the naming of Manasseh we saw Joseph still standing, as it were, on the border between Jew and Gentile, between Egypt and Canaan, between the home of his childhood and the kingdom that God had put into his hands when he became a man. "God hath caused me to forget," he said; and yet he had not quite forgotten "all his toil, and all his father's house" (see Gen. 41:51). In the birth of Ephraim a little later, he speaks as a Gentile. "God hath caused me to be fruitful in the land of my affliction" (v. 52).

Ephraim is the fruitfulness of his father in the land of Egypt as a Gentile prince; and Jacob rightly calls his seed "the fullness of the Gentiles" (see Gen. 48:19), when he adopts him on his dying bed. Accordingly, we cannot be surprised at the position in Old Testament history which Ephraim receives. He is the rival of Judah as long as any rivalry can last. Judah marched at the head of the first half of the camp in the wilderness; Ephraim headed the second half. Judah's camp lay at the eastern side of the tabernacle; the camp of Ephraim was pitched upon the west. The two will be united hereafter, when Ezekiel's prophecy shall come to pass; and "the stick of Ephraim shall be joined to the stick of Judah, and one king shall again be king over all Israel in their own land" (Ezek. 37:16-22).

110

I do not know anything which is more assuring as to the truth of that view of prophecy which requires the restoration of God's ancient people, than the comparison between the history of Ephraim and the prophecies that are written about him in the Old Testament. It seems so certain that there are things written about Ephraim which cannot yet have been fulfilled. That very prophecy of Ezekiel's is an example. It was written after all the kings of Israel and Judah had passed away. There has been no king over all Israel since except the Herods, who were certainly not promised as a blessing to the people by their prophets. There must yet be one king in that land over Israel and Judah if the prophecy is to come true.

We must endeavor to sketch the history of the tribe of Ephraim, in order to see what answers to it spiritually among the people of God. The birthright of Reuben was given to the sons of Joseph; and Ephraim being set before Manasseh, took the chief place. This gave him a claim to be lord over his brethren; but God chose the tribe of Judah to be first of all.

Yet there is a kind of alternation between Ephraim and Judah from beginning to end. Joseph was his father's favorite among the children (Gen. 37:3), but at the proposal of Judah, Joseph was sold into Egypt for a slave (vv. 26-27). Then Joseph became lord over all Egypt, and next to Pharaoh (41:41); and we see Judah interceding for Benjamin and offering to be a slave to Joseph himself (44:18-34). Judah is chosen to lead the hosts of Israel in the wilderness (Num. 2:9); but Joshua, a man of the tribe of Ephraim, heads the armies of Israel in the passage of Jordan and the conquest of the land (Josh. 1:1-2). The tabernacle is set up at Shiloh (Josh. 18:1), and the chief town of Israel is Shechem—both situated in the tribe of Ephraim. But Shiloh is laid desolate (Ps. 78:60); Jerusalem is preferred to Shechem; and Judah becomes the royal tribe.

Ephraim contends for the first place throughout the government of the judges, but is not able to keep the lead. Yet again, Ephraim rebels against the king in Jerusalem, and succeeds at last in establishing a kingdom of ten tribes (1 Ki. 12:20). Solomon reigned in Jerusalem, and built the temple there. But his son Rehoboam was

111

compelled to go to Shechem in Mount Ephraim, and deal with Israel for the throne (12:1). The kingdom of the ten tribes was swept away about 130 years before Jerusalem was taken by Nebuchadnezzar; and the kings of Judah reigned over the remnant that was left in the land. Then Judah also went into captivity, and ever since the Jews have been one people until now.[1] But the whole Jewish race was at last rejected for the time, and the Gentiles, of whom Ephraim's seed was to be the fullness, received the gospel, and seem to hold the light of the world. Now we are again expecting the twelve tribes to be restored. Thus the alternatings between Ephraim and Judah continue throughout history and prophecy from first to last.

The representative man of the tribe of Ephraim is Joshua. No one like him arose afterwards in that tribe. Jeroboam, the son of Nebat, the founder of the kingdom of Ephraim, was the opposite of Joshua in every way. Joshua was "the shepherd and stone of Israel" (Gen. 49:24) in early days. He established the people in the land. Jeroboam, the son of Nebat, "made Israel to sin" (1 Ki. 16:26; 21:22), and the sin proved incurable. "The Lord gave Israel up" (2 Chron. 30:7; Ps. 81:12) and rejected them, for the worship of Jeroboam's golden calves. Joshua and Jeroboam led the tribe of Ephraim at its best and at its worst. Jeroboam was the sinner and the stumbling-block. The very name of Joshua was made for Him who "shall save His people from their sins" (Mt. 1:21).

Jeroboam and Joshua represent the chief fault and the chief excellence of Ephraim in another way. I think no one will doubt that the chief characteristic of Joshua is humility. This goes so far that the difficulty is to detect any character at all. We know the meaning of

1. The common expression, "The lost ten tribes," is based on a misconception. The kingdom of Israel was never restored at Samaria, but there is no evidence that any tribe ever lost its identity or was merged in the Gentiles. There is abundant evidence in Scripture to the contrary. After the destruction of Jerusalem by Titus, the genealogies appear to have perished, and now no tribe can be distinguished. But a Jew can be distinguished from a Gentile, and always could.

Joshua's name, Jehovah-Saviour, we know his position under Moses, and his work as leader of Israel. His jealous affection for his master appeared when he would have his lord Moses forbid the two elders who prophesied in the camp without going forth to the tabernacle (Num. 11:28-29). His jealousy for the honor of his God breaks forth in the last address to the people at Shechem, when he bids them choose for themselves whom they shall worship, but adds, "as for me and my house, we will serve Jehovah" (Josh. 24:15). But Joshua never puts himself forward, even in his mightiest deeds. It is the work, not the man, that attracts attention.

Some have thought him a naturally timid and retiring character. The words so often repeated at the beginning of his career, "Be strong and of a good courage" (Josh. 1:6, 9, 18), seem to point to this. His extreme depression after the defeat of Israel before Ai is an indication of the same kind. On that occasion God seems almost to rebuke him, "Get thee up; wherefore liest thou thus upon thy face? Israel hath sinned" (7:10-11). Every reader must have noticed the gentleness of his words to Achan, the troubler of Israel, when the lot had fallen on him. "My son, give, I pray thee, glory to the Lord God of Israel, and make confession unto Him; and tell me now what thou hast done; hide it not from me" (Josh. 7:19). At no time was the tribe of Ephraim so highly exalted as it was when Joshua was its head.

Another little incident recorded of Joshua shows his humility. Not until all the twelve tribes had received their inheritance did Joshua ask anything for himself (Josh. 19:49-50). Timnath Serah, "a portion that remaineth," or "a portion of a remnant," was what he asked. But at his death we find its name changed in the book of Judges, and it has become Timnath Heres, "Portion of the sun" (see Judg. 2:9). One cannot but pay attention to the name of Joshua's city, and the record of his burial, when we know Whose name he bore, and of Whom he was the figure. The very name of his city was reversed after his burial, and underwent a kind of resurrection from the dead, reminding us of Him, whose last resting-place on earth became the scene of His greatest glory, when He arose as the Sun of Righteousness, and robbed death of its sting.

If all Ephraim's leaders had been men of the character of Joshua, the history of the tribe would have been very different. "When Ephraim spake trembling, he exalted himself in Israel; but when he offended in Baal, he died" (Hos. 13:1). But "woe to the crown of pride, the drunkards of Ephraim, whose glorious beauty is a fading flower! The crown of pride, the drunkards of Ephraim, shall be trodden under feet" (Isa. 28:1, 3). The pride that led Ephraim to separate from the house of Judah, ensnared the tribe into idolatry, and made the separation complete. "Ephraim is joined to idols: let him alone" (Hos. 4:17). The line of the kings of Israel does not belong to the tribe of Ephraim. Jeroboam's son, Nadab, was the last king known to be of that family. Baasha, who cut off the house of Jeroboam, was a man of Issachar; and after the death of Baasha and his son Elah, it is impossible to say to what tribe the kings of Israel belonged. The kingdom went into captivity; and the kings of Assyria peopled the cities of Ephraim with idolaters, who mixed the worship of idols with the worship of the God of Israel, and were the forefathers of the Samaritans of the time of our Lord.

A certain remnant of Ephraim and Israel united itself with Judah, and returned to Jerusalem in the reign of Cyrus. But Samaria and Shechem, and Shiloh, where Joshua and the children of Israel established the government and the worship of God, have long been separated from all association with God's people. The Samaritans of New Testament history always seem more like Gentiles than Jews.

The prophecies addressed to Israel as distinct from Judah would point first to Ephraim, the acknowledged head of the ten tribes. Pride of our own privileges is our danger as well as Ephraim's, according to the caution addressed to us by Paul in the famous passage where he shows the position of Jew and Gentile in the good olive tree of God. "Boast not against the branches...Be not high-minded; but fear" (Rom. 11:18, 20). The God who punished Israel for the sin of Ephraim will punish us also for our pride.

But the pride of Ephraim in the days of his power in Israel receives a most significant rebuke in the list of the sealed tribes in the Revelation. His name is simply omitted—he gives place to his father Joseph, whose children were to be called after the name of Ephraim and Manasse in their inheritance. The name of the humble Joshua has risen above every name; the name of the proud Ephraim is lost; for "every one that exalteth himself shall be abased, and he that humbleth himself shall be exalted" (Mt. 23:12). The chief city of Ephraim was shut out of Israel for many generations as unclean.

But may we not take such portions of Old Testament Scripture as the prophecy of Hosea, which speaks more especially of Ephraim and Israel, as also applying to the churches? In Jeremiah 31:31, we find that a new covenant is made with the house of Israel and with the house of Judah. Perhaps Israel is named first because of her ancient link with the Gentiles, and that the new covenant was accepted in the first instance by the Gentile rather than the Jew. It is not yet accepted by the children of Abraham, though it is dear to the hearts of the spiritual sons of Abraham (Rom. 4:11).

There is no mention of Ephraim in Revelation, but we cannot therefore conclude that the tribe is not redeemed. Of the tribe of Joseph as well as of Manasseh were sealed 12,000. There is room for Ephraim there, and who can count the multitude that may pass through the gate of Joseph into the golden city? The name Joseph signifies Jehovah's addition,[2] "Jehovah shall add to me another son" (Gen. 30:24). So long as the Lord is adding to the multitude of the saved, the gate of Joseph is open, his tribe increasing, his number not yet exhausted, his name unfulfilled. And however many the Lord shall add to the multitude of His Israel, they must all be added in one way: the multitude is made up of those "who have washed their robes and made them white in the blood of the Lamb. Therefore are they before the throne of God."

2. From the form Jehoseph in the Hebrew of Psalm 81:5, we gather that Joseph was a contraction, and that a portion of the name Jehovah was included in the original name.

14
BENJAMIN

Benjamin shall ravin as a wolf: in the morning he shall devour the
prey, and at night he shall divide the spoil.
GENESIS 49:27

And of Benjamin he said, The beloved of the Lord shall dwell in
safety by him; and the Lord shall cover him all the day long, and he
shall dwell between his shoulders.
DEUTERONOMY 33:12

The tribe of Benjamin is the last, the bravest, and the best-beloved
of all the tribes of Israel, the center of the affections of the whole
family, and the dwelling-place of the beloved of the Lord.

The prophecy of Jacob regarding him is short and easily verified:
"Benjamin shall ravin as a wolf: in the morning he shall devour the
prey, and at night he shall divide the spoil."

The first feature in this description is personal courage. This is
characteristic of the Benjamites throughout history. The second of
the judges of Israel, Ehud, who delivered his people from the
Moabite, gave an example of it in the deed by which he effected their
deliverance, acting on his own responsibility, single-handed, and of

his own accord. The sword with which he slew Eglon was of his own making. To bring it concealed upon his person into the king's presence, as he seems to have done twice over, and the second time alone, that he might risk no other life in Israel if he failed, was an act of no small daring on his part, and was crowned with success (see Judg. 3).

A little later, the tribe of Benjamin proved itself a match for all Israel in the terrible conflict, which might have been averted if the Benjamites had been willing to surrender a few guilty inhabitants of a single town. In the first two days of that terrible battle, though the odds against them were nearly 15 to 1, the Benjamites slew more of the fighting men of Israel than the whole number of the warriors of their own tribe. Gibeah was at last taken by stratagem; but even then there was no surrender. The 600 who escaped of Benjamin abode three months in the rock Rimmon until the tribes of Israel relented and called them back (see Judg. 19, 20, 21).

After this exhibition of courage in the least of the tribes, we cannot be surprised that when God chose a king to suit the desire of the people, Saul of Gibeah was His choice. They wished for a king to fight their battles. Where were they likely to find a braver leader than in Benjamin? In this they were not disappointed. "From the blood of the slain, from the fat of the mighty, the bow of Jonathan turned not back, and the sword of Saul returned not empty" (2 Sam. 1:22). Even in his faults the courage of Saul is characteristic. He was not immune to temptation—he feared the people and obeyed their voice; but on the wolf-like courage of Benjamin he has left no stain.

Jonathan's entire history exhibits the character of Benjamin under the influence of divine grace, and there is no lovelier character in the whole of Old Testament history than his. The courage of Benjamin was well displayed when Jonathan raised the standard of insurrection against the Philistines by smiting their garrison in Geba, thus commencing the war (1 Sam. 13:3). A second garrison in Michmash he attacked with no other comrade except his armor-bearer, and this at a moment where it was doubtful whether the people had sufficient spirit to follow up a successful attack (14:1-23). Jonathan's boldness was, however, an important step to success. Again and again did he brave his father's anger for the sake of David, to the risk of his own life, and died at last fighting bravely in the cause of Israel, though he might have foreseen what would happen, and saved himself with David, if he would (1 Sam. 31:2).

The only men who dared to show themselves in open antagonism to David when he became king (except his son Absalom) were Benjamites: Abner first (2 Sam. 2:14-17), and afterwards Shimei the son of Gera (16:5-13), and Sheba the son of Bichri (ch. 20). The wolf-like courage of Benjamin was displayed again here. The resistance of Mordecai to Haman the king's favorite at the Persian court (Est. 3:2-6), his faithful denunciation of the conspirators, with Esther's boldness in entering the king's presence uncalled (4:16), for the sake of her people, all maintained the character of Benjamin. And if Simeon smote the remnant of the Amalekites, Israel's earliest foe, it was reserved for Benjamin to destroy the royal family of Agag and bring the dangerous quarrel to a close (9:24-26).

The same personal courage is manifested to the fullest extent in the great Benjamite persecutor and apostle, Saul of Tarsus, later the apostle Paul. He made havoc of the Church like a wolf, in the persecution. And there is no adequate comparison to express his endurance in the good fight of faith. His personal sufferings in the defense of the gospel are unparalleled. It is no slight testimony to his courage that he should have been permitted so often to imperil the cause that was bound up with his safety, and to maintain it without human bid. The Lord stood with him, and "strengthened" him (2 Tim. 4:17). But what other man did the Lord honor by leaving him to fight so sore a conflict unrelieved and unaided, except by His enduring grace? Others have been delivered from danger and suffering; Paul was left to fight his way through that he might become a monument of the power of Christ.

The case of Paul brings us naturally to the second part of Jacob's prophecy: "In the morning he shall devour the prey, and at night he shall divide the spoil." This also finds abundant illustration in the narrative. Benjamin devoured Israel in the morning by the war at Gibeah, at night in persecution by Saul. Paul also divided the spoil

119

with his brother-apostles, laboring more abundantly than they all (see 1 Cor. 15:10). Who else was the means of winning so many souls to Christ?

In the morning of Israel's kingdom, Saul of Benjamin sat on Israel's throne (1 Sam. 9:15-16). In the night of the dispersion, Esther of Benjamin was Queen of Persia, bearing sway over 127 provinces from Africa to India (Est. 2:17).

There are only two Benjamites who left a stain on the face of the family—Ishbosheth (2 Sam. 2–4) and Mephibosheth (4:2).[1] The fact that they did disgrace it is marked by the shameful appendage to their names. There is probably another reason for the change from Baal to Bosheth, but unless it had been felt that the honor of the tribe was tarnished, Scripture would scarcely have stereotyped the change.

The principal fact indicated by the blessing of Moses, that in Benjamin is the dwelling of the Lord's beloved, seems to foretell that Jerusalem, the beloved city, would be in the inheritance of this tribe. The glory of Benjamin has here been obscured by Judah; "Judah prevailed above his brethren, and of him came the chief ruler" (1 Chron. 5:2). Judah had the lion's share in the capture of Jerusalem. The suburbs, and perhaps even a portion of the city itself, were in Judah's inheritance. In any case, a city which Judah shared with Benjamin would soon be accounted the property of the greater tribe.

But the rights of the case must be decided by a reference to Joshua. In the division of the land, as he records it, Jerusalem has been assigned to Benjamin, and there the right must remain (Josh. 18:28). Perhaps the expression of the Psalmist, "There is little Benjamin their ruler" (Ps. 68:27), may partly refer to this fact. There, "between the shoulders" of Benjamin, the God of Israel caused His name to dwell. In Benjamin He "covered Israel all the day long" (Deut. 33:2). "As birds flying, so did the Lord of hosts defend

---

1. Originally Esh-baal and Merib-baal. Baal, i.e., Lord; Baheth, i.e., shame. There is some question as to who was telling the truth to David—Mephibosheth or his servant—when David returned to Jerusalem after being driven away by Absalom.

Jerusalem" (Isa. 31:5). There He "would often have gathered her children together, even as a hen doth gather her brood under her wings, but they would not!" (Lk. 13:34). Benjamin would still ravin as a wolf. "Jerusalem, Jerusalem, that killest the prophets, and stonest them that are sent unto thee!" (Mt. 23:37). "It cannot be that a prophet perish out of Jerusalem!" (Lk. 13:33). This was the return that the city of Benjamin made to the Lord for His protection. It was the one place in Israel where neither the Lord Himself nor His prophets could be safe. "They took Him, and cast Him out of the city, and slew Him" (Acts 7:58), is the oft-repeated record of His servants' end.

Not inaptly did Joseph give commandment that his silver cup should be placed in Benjamin's sack. It is in his inheritance that the cup of life is found. "Of him must be required all the righteous blood shed upon the earth" (Mt. 23:35), from the first page of God's book of martyrs to the last.[2] Judah may well give himself up for the guilt attaching to his brother, but the cup is found in Benjamin's sack; nor could it have been put there unless the true Joseph had consented there to die.

When the shedding of that righteous blood is acknowledged and forgiven, Benjamin will become the meeting-place of all Israel, the center of affection of all the tribes. This affection has been illustrated in many ways already. Jacob would not let Benjamin go till the lives of all his children were at stake (Gen. 43:8-14). Joseph would not admit his brethren to his presence, unless Benjamin came with them (v. 3). All Israel wept for Benjamin when the tribe was so nearly cut off (Judg. 21:6). Personal affection and tenderness seems to

---

2. The blood of Abel stands first, for obvious reasons. The blood of Zacharias is last, probably because it is the last mentioned in the Old Testament. In the Hebrew Bible, the books of Chronicles are placed last. Thus Zacharias is a representative person, and stands for the last martyr in the Book. To a Jew, "From Abel to Zacharias" would be as natural an expression as "from Dan to Beersheba." We have the books in a different order, and therefore are perplexed. See 2 Chron. 24:21.

have been a characteristic of the Benjamites from the first. Joseph kissed all his brethren, and wept upon them. Benjamin wept upon his neck (Gen. 45:14), though his personal knowledge of his brother must have been least among them all. Saul's strong affection breaks out again and again, as often as he is released from the spirit of jealousy by that influence of David's words. Jonathan's love for his friend was "wonderful, passing the love of women" (2 Sam. 1:26). The patriotism of Esther and Mordecai springs from the same root; and in the life of Paul, no characteristic as more remarkable than his wonderful tenderness and affection for all with whom he had to do. He was the only man whose heart was large enough to die for the Jewish nation and for the Gentile world. He would have been "accursed from Christ for his brethren" (Rom. 9:3). For the liberty of Gentile Christians, he was "in deaths oft" (2 Cor. 11:23).

There may be some difficulty in showing how the virtues and vices of Benjamin can be the expression of the same character, even under opposite influences. But the ruling principle seems to be impulsiveness. The object of Benjamin's desire is pursued without the least regard to consequences. The cruelties and vices of the Benjamites were the indulgence of unbridled passion. Their virtues were the expression of undaunted love. Saul casting javelins at David (1 Sam. 18:11); saving the men of Jabesh-Gilead by a sudden appeal to all Israel (ch. 11); sentencing the priests to death, and even his son Jonathan too, in a moment of passion; yet bursting into tears at the sound of the voice of David (24:16); utterly overcome by the terrible apparition at Endor (28:20); and yet fighting bravely to the last (ch. 31). Who does not see that he is the creature of impulse throughout?

The effect of divine grace is to control the outward expression of these impulses, but not to chill the loving heart from which they spring. We see this exhibited in Jonathan and Paul. The result is a kind of deliberate passion in God's service, which produces an almost unconquerable force. The conversion of Paul by a sudden onset of divine love and glory, exhibits God's way of dealing with this character for good. Probably the behavior of the persecuted disciples had given many a prick already to the warm, but misguided heart. The behavior of Christians under persecution would have an influence that a man of Benjamin would find it hard to withstand.

The tribe of Benjamin, as the seat of God's love, ought to be the meeting-point for all Israel; Jerusalem is so, in a figure. It has open gates for all the tribes of Israel, and "is built as a city that is at unity in itself. Thither the tribes go up, even the tribes of the Lord" (see Ps. 122:4). For a little while it held Israel together under David and Solomon. Perhaps as the religious center of the twelve tribes dispersed after the Babylonish captivity, it was more successful. Still, however, the bitter quarrel between Jews and Samaritans remained. The feud in Paul's time between the circumcision and uncircumcision was not reconciled. Even his influence, with the preaching and the practice of the "charity that never faileth" (1 Cor. 13:8), could not accomplish the task. Like Abner, the great Benjamite general, Paul had made a league with the true David; and his hand would have been with Him to bring about all Israel unto their king; but the lives of both were cut off before they could accomplish their purpose.

If Paul was the true fulfillment of Benjamin's destiny, his birth was his mother's death. The Jews regarded him as her Ben-oni, the son of her sorrow; though he was his father's right hand. She has never borne another apostle since. The last fulfillment of this history will bring us to the re-appearance of the true Joseph. "At the second time," when "Joseph is made known unto his brethren" (see Gen. 4:1), the twelve tribes of Israel will be united in Benjamin for evermore.

15
THE ORDER OF THE SEALED TRIBES

And I heard the number of them which were sealed:
and there were sealed an hundred and forty and four thousand
of all the tribes of the children of Israel.
REVELATION 7:4

There is a remarkable order and principle in the arrangement of the twelve tribes in this chapter of Revelation. The list here given is the last in Scripture where the names occur. And the twelve names given are all in pairs. The arrangement of these pairs suggests some interesting thoughts about the possible results of earthly training and discipline, in the meeting of God's children hereafter around the throne of God. Anything that casts light on the connection between earth and heaven in this way is too precious to be lost.

A glance at the order of the names before us will show the pairs:

1. Judah and Reuben.
2. Gad and Asher.
3. Naphtali and Manasseh.
4. Simeon and Levi.
5. Issachar and Zebulun.
6. Joseph and Benjamin.

One could not believe that this arrangement is accidental. There is no greater mistake than to suppose that anything in God's Word can be accidental, any more than there is anything outside the range of His providence in His works. Of both alike it is true, that "without Him was not anything made that was made" (Jn. 1:3). And surely the order of names in this place where God's mark is finally set on the tribes of Israel, may be taken to indicate in some degree their position before His throne. What members of God's family shall stand next to each other in the life to come? Could there be a more interesting question than this?

Judah is of course first, and Reuben is next to Judah in the first pair. The Lion of the tribe of Judah, the root and offspring of David, must raise that tribe to the head of all. Reuben was the firstborn and lost the birthright, and gave place to the sons of Joseph; Ephraim took the birthright, and was above Reuben all through their life together as children of Israel in this present evil world. But where is Ephraim in this list in Revelation? The name is not to be found. Ephraim joined himself to idols, and made Israel to sin. He held not fast that which he had and, now, Reuben has retaken his crown.

Where else could Reuben have been in any case but second? He could not have been before Judah, if Judah was to be the tribe of our Lord. We may well believe that Reuben's sin is forgiven and forgotten—blotted out of the book of remembrance, according to the covenant, "Their sins and their iniquities I will remember no more" (Heb. 8:12). The sentence of Jacob upon Reuben, "Thou shalt not excel," is executed, and its force is now spent; only the prayer of the mediator is remembered, "Let Reuben live, and not die."

The intensely human character of Judah and the versatility of Reuben are well matched. Both had natural excellence in everything. Judah had the decision to use his abilities from the first. Reuben gained that talent only by long and hard discipline. But see, it is gained at last, and the two brothers are sealed together with the seal of the living God. That fixes their character and stamps them permanently with His image. No longer shall they sin and come short of the glory of God.

126

Gad and Asher, who come next, were brothers, the sons of one mother, Zilpah, Leah's handmaid; sons of the bondwoman, they were made children of Israel by adoption, and, being closely united by nature, there was no reason why they should be separated by their heavenly birth.

We may remark in their history that, in both cases, the position they occupied was more noticeable than their character, and yet the character was suited to their position in the land. Gad was blessed by Moses in these terms, "Blessed be he that enlargeth Gad: he dwelleth as a lion, and teareth the arm with the crown of the head. And he provided the first part for himself, because there, in a portion of the lawgiver, was he seated." It is fitting that he who had the first portion and inheritance from Moses should stand so high in the list. You remember how he was shut in between the Jordan on one side and the Ammonites on the other, in the mountains of Gilead. You remember the troops that were to overcome him, and how he was to overcome at the last. Behold, he has gained the victory! He is now sealed next to Judah and Reuben, with the seal of the living God. In a land beset with enemies, he dwelt as a lion and often sheltered the outcasts of Israel in his mountain fortresses.

But who would have thought to see his brother so close beside him at the last? Asher, that remained so quietly by the seashore and abiding in the creeks, living at peace in a rich inheritance, and scarcely ever lifting a finger for war. How can he have come hither?

In his place of abode, Asher was as remarkable for avoiding conflicts as Gad was for his readiness to meet a foe. But they were brothers first and last. Asher went up to Jerusalem to the mountain of the Lord's house and dwelt there, and then at last, in the days of our Saviour, found a voice to speak of Him to those that expected redemption in Jerusalem. The house of the Lord is at least as high a dwelling-place as the mountains of Gilead. One tribe may witness for Him in the place of battle, another may find it as hard to testify for Him in the abodes of peace. From distant regions and by very different experiences, Gad and his brother Asher found their way to meet at last. If Gad was first in the portion of the Lawgiver, in the Old

127

Covenant, Asher was first in the portion of the Gospel-giver in the New Covenant. Both at last came to dwell together in the New Jerusalem; the one escaped from the bondage of the enemy, and the other from the bondage of self. The one was made conqueror over a troop of foes from without, the other victorious over slothfulness within. We may learn here that very opposite dispositions and very different experiences in the career of brothers in this life need not part them in the life to come.

Naphtali and Manasseh come next. This is the combination that would be most difficult to explain without the history; all the others are obvious, if we can explain this.

Naphtali is peculiarly situated in this list. His own brother was Dan, and Dan is missing altogether. With whom could Naphtali be placed? His mother was Bilhah, Rachel's handmaid. Manasseh was the eldest grandson of Rachel, the one whose position (after Dan) comes nearest to Naphtali. His brother Ephraim is missing, too. Only one son of Rachel's handmaid Bilhah, and one son of her son Joseph are in this list. Is it strange that the two should be placed together?

Naphtali and Manasseh were both connected in their prophetic history with the preaching of the gospel. It is Naphtali that gives goodly words, like a hind let loose upon the mountains. For the same purpose Manasseh is divided, and forgets the things that are behind. Each of these tribes may be said to have forsaken home, and risked life for the service of the gospel, Naphtali taking the lead.

Both are cut off from home and kindred. Manasseh is left without his younger brother Ephraim, Naphtali without his older brother Dan, in the house of Israel. The two solitary brothers are united in God's service. Naphtali, a younger brother, finds in Manasseh, an elder brother, a compensation for his loss. And yet, as Manasseh gave place to his younger brother Ephraim, so he lets Naphtali take the lead. Can it be by accident that these two bereaved ones are found together in God's family? Is it not He that "setteth the solitary in families" (Ps. 68:6), especially if they have become solitary for Him? There is nothing more beautiful in the whole passage than the uniting of these two bereaved and lonely brothers in the Israel of God.

About the three last pairs there will be no difficulty. Simeon and Levi come next. Why not? Simeon and Levi came close together, second and third among the sons of Leah, and were they not united by the closest affection from the first? They stood together in enterprises until they were providentially forced to part. "Simeon and Levi are brethren," said their father on his dying bed. He cursed their wrath and anger, divided them in Jacob, and scattered them in Israel. We have observed the hard life of Simeon, the diminution of the tribe, his separation first from Levi, then from his companions in the wilderness, then from all his brethren except Judah, in whose inheritance he at last found a home. But, like Levi, Simeon learned a lesson in the loneliness of his career on earth. The two that Jacob parted came together again at last—they received the seal of God together, and are brothers at home in heaven, where they part no more. The priestly office of Levi seems forgotten here, where all are kings and priests to God, but many a one would give up all his earthly offices and honors if he might again be united with those whom he has loved. There is sufficient compensation for all such losses in the fact that Simeon and Levi are joined again.

Issachar and Zebulun are the next, and they also were close together—fifth and sixth—among the sons of Leah. They were never parted on earth; and see, they are not parted in heaven! Side by side they marched under Judah's banner in the wilderness. Side by side they dwelt together in the Promised Land. Moses blessed them with one blessing, only distinguishing their shares in the work before them, work which means the preaching of the gospel abroad and at home. "Rejoice, Zebulun, in thy going out; and, Issachar, in thy tents." What if Zebulun seems to have been poor and warlike, Issachar, on the contrary, rich and wise? The poverty of the one was exalted by the dwelling of the Saviour at Nazareth; the wisdom of the other had been mere time-serving, unless Issachar had been redeemed and elevated by that same Lord. There need not be any parting, either on earth or in heaven, between those who are born together into the family of God.

Last of all come Joseph and Benjamin, the two children of Rachel,

129

the beloved of their father, whose separation brought such sorrow upon Jacob, whose meeting together was the reunion of the whole house. Where else could they be, except together?

They come last, being the two youngest; and yet not that reason only. Take this list, just as it stands, clasp the two ends together like a bracelet, and what do you find? You will have fitted Benjamin into Judah, putting him just where he was in the land of Israel, to be the link between Judah and Joseph, and the center of the whole family, as he always was. The circle stands completed around the throne; six pairs of tribes are there, and now what remains?

One pair of names is missing—Dan and Ephraim. These were the two that made Israel to sin. A man of Mount Ephraim, whose name was Micah, made the graven images and consecrated the priest that the children of Dan took away and established all the time that God's house was in Shiloh (see Judg. 17–18). King Jeroboam set up his golden calves, the one in Bethel and the other in Dan—Bethel being then a city of Ephraim, taken from Benjamin, of whom Joshua gave it at first (see 1 Ki. 12:28-29). The two tribes that are absent are a pair, as their brothers Naphtali and Manasseh are a pair. The two first forsook God for idols; the others forsook everything for God.

We need not suppose that the tribes of Dan and Ephraim have perished. Dan was counted to the house of Joseph in the earliest days of the Judges, and Ephraim may very well have taken shelter under Joseph's wing. Doubtless the tribe of Joseph may include members of both these; but still the point is made good, that they who lead others into sin shall not go unpunished (Ex. 34:7). If "they that be wise" (like Issachar) "shall shine as the brightness of that firmament, and they that turn many to righteousness" (like Zebulun) "as the stars for ever and ever" (Dan. 12:3), it is no less true that they that forsake the Lord shall perish, and they that depart from Him "shall be written in the earth" (Jer. 17:13). "The destruction of the transgressors and of the sinners shall be together, and they that forsake the Lord shall be consumed" (Isa. 1:28).

The disappearance of Ephraim's name also enforces another lesson—that "He that exalteth himself shall be abased" (Mt. 23:12). No other tribe in all Israel was so incessantly maintaining his position, insisting upon the payment of the honor due to his name; and in this last record the name is simply left out! Instead of being first, where Ephraim would have put it, it is not there at all. Joseph is reinstated, and Ephraim is reminded that he owes his whole existence in Israel to his father's name. "What hast thou that thou didst not receive? Now, if thou didst receive it, why dost thou glory, as though thou hadst not received it?" (1 Cor. 4:7).

Dan, too, was a great leader in Israel, and in the Exodus he was second to none but Judah in his strength. But "many that are first shall be last" (Mt. 19:30), and so in this case. This was not "the honor that cometh from God only" (Jn. 5:44).

Enough has now been said to show that the order of these tribes most certainly follows an assignable principle, though what that principle is we have not fully explained. That they are in pairs is undeniable, and the first and the last pair could not be anywhere else. But why Gad and Asher should come before Naphtali and Manasseh—and Simeon and Levi, and Issachar and Zebulun after them—is a question that still remains unanswered.

However, one remarkable feature must not escape our notice. In no single instance has the tie of natural relationship been disregarded here. Judah and Reuben had the same mother; Gad and Asher were the only children of the same mother; Simeon and Levi brethren, next in age, sons of one mother; Issachar and Zebulun, next to each other also, both sons of Leah; Joseph and Benjamin, the only children of Rachel. Naphtali and Manasseh are less closely united, but each of them had lost his own brother, and neither of them had any nearer relations in the same generation among these twelve names. Peculiar circumstances also fitted them to be together.

Is there not something in all this to rebuke the faithless notion so common among Christians, that the necessities of heaven must dislocate the family ties of earth? If I had only one brother whose life on earth was very short, who never gave anything but a child's testimony to the truth of God, and he has been with Christ these many years, while I have been left here to run the common race must we therefore necessarily be separated in God's service in the world to come? If we are both members of the true family of God, when we come to the Father's house, why should we be compelled to part?

I was always taught to look forward to heaven as a meeting-place. Some persons, regarding only the difference between natural and spiritual relationships, make heaven a place of parting, where we are to be grouped and classified according to our attainments, and never see one another, except in the distance, anymore. It seems to me to argue a very low idea of God's power of organization, to suppose that He cannot bring together those whom He has led by different ways. At all events, this list of the tribes sealed by God does not look like parting at the last. Several most remarkable instances of the preservation of natural relationship have been shown to us; we find not one violent separation of those who are naturally united, where both are truly members of the Israel of God.

Surely this may encourage us to cling to the Rock of Israel, and trust in Him. Surely He will "build up Jerusalem and gather together the outcasts of Israel, heal the broken in heart, and bind up their wounds" (see Ps. 147:2-3), and make compensation that shall be truly wonderful for all that has been spoiled and disunited in this world of sin and sorrow. "He shall redeem Israel from all his troubles" and "all iniquities," if Israel will only humble himself to be redeemed (see Ps. 25:22; 130:8).

And certainly the order of the twelve tribes in Israel, named in the beginning of this seventh chapter of Revelation, is not to be separated from what follows: "After this I beheld, and, lo, a great multitude, which no man can number..." Doubtless we may understand that all these are sealed with the seal of the living God, as well as the tribes of Israel; and if the final arrangement of those twelve tribes bears marks of such loving care and design on God's part, and harmonizes so remarkably with their former history, may we not expect the same love and care, and perfect order, in the arrangement of all the countless multitude of the redeemed? All that believe in God, through Jesus Christ, are the children of Abraham. He has given us the twelve tribes of Israel for a pattern: All things that befell them "happened to them for ensamples, and are written for our admonition" (1 Cor. 10:11). We have clear ground for this view of their history, that they were made "types of us." The same God and Father is over all; the same redemption is for all; the same kind of training and preparation is appointed to us in this life, and we have the same kind of expectation for the life to come. What else but the fact that this example and pattern is given us in Scripture would have justified this attempt to trace the separate history of the twelve tribes? Will not their experience encourage us to hope for many a similar reunion in the "great multitude that no man can number, of all nations, and kindreds, and people, and tongues"?

Appendix

THE BOUNDS
OF THE NATIONS

We are told that "when the most High divided to the nations their inheritance, when He separated the sons of Adam, He set the bounds of the people according to the number of the children of Israel" (Deut. 32:8). The portion of Genesis called "the generations of the sons of Noah" (Gen. 10:1-11:9) gives us an account of that separation. It tells us where the various descendants of Noah had their inheritance, and how they were separated—Japheth here, Ham there, and Shem elsewhere.

It also tells us that they were violently separated in the days of Peleg at Babel by the confusion of tongues. It was certainly the work of the "Most High." It was the Lord who "separated the sons of Adam," when they were determined not to separate themselves. God had provided their inheritance. He had bidden them to "be fruitful and multiply and replenish the earth." But they would not obey His law until He made them differ in language, so that separate nations might be formed in every corner of the world, and that all man's various powers might be developed, according to the varied necessities of his environment.

We learn in Deuteronomy that these various nations in every quarter of the earth received their inheritance with reference to another

135

nation not then formed, "He set the bounds of the people according to the number of the children of Israel."

Paul, in his speech at Athens, made a statement which looks very like a comment on this. God "made of one blood all nations of men for to dwell on all the face of the earth, and determined times before appointed, and the setting of the bounds of their habitation; that they should seek the Lord, if haply they might feel after Him, and find Him, though He be not far from every one of us" (Acts 17:26-27).

In both places we read of the dispersion of the nations, and in both we find the rule which modified that dispersion.

Surely the one statement throws light on the other. When the bounds of each nation were determined, and the times that should pass over it, i.e., the various changes and periods in its history, when these things were determined by the Most High, He Himself tells us that He considered two things: the number of the children of Israel; and how the other nations might have an opportunity to seek the Lord. This is the general truth indicated.

It is not easy to discover how far it extends. We can only follow the working of it within certain limits, and wait for the disclosure of what we cannot see about the rest. However, the outlines of the plan in sacred history are enough to suggest the whole. The opportunities given to the nations mentioned in the Old Testament, through their contact with the seed of Abraham, are not difficult to trace.

When Abram and Lot walked together through the land of Canaan and built altars to the Lord, "the Canaanite and the Perizzite dwelled then in the land." When Abram went down into Egypt, his presence there brought a visitation from God on Pharaoh, and compelled him to pay attention to the divine law. It was the same when Abram went to the king of the Philistines, who also was brought into communion with Jehovah, and obtained a blessing through the patriarch's prayers.

When Joseph was sold into Egypt, the providence of God was even more strikingly displayed. The whole nation was brought under the sway of Jacob's chosen son. It was not possible that the people should be completely under Joseph's government and yet be ignorant of Joseph's God.

And when the king arose who "knew not Joseph," and oppressed Israel, the visitations of God that followed certainly accomplished the desired end. What that end was we may find on almost any page of the narrative of the plagues of Egypt. "The Egyptians shall know that I am the Lord." It was not much that they knew perhaps. But how little was known even by the mass of the Israelites? When Joshua had established them in Canaan, it was very little that he required of them in his farewell charge, "To put away the strange gods and serve Jehovah, and to remember that He was not only a mighty, but a holy God." This was the last charge of Joshua. It would not be difficult for other nations to find out from Israel as much as the mass of Israelites knew themselves.

When they were marching in the wilderness, the impression produced on the nations around them was by no means slight. Take the story of Balaam on the one hand, and the confession of Rahab on the other. On both sides of Jordan there was the strongest impression of the power of Israel's God.

Balaam's prophecy to Balak could not have been uttered without leaving an impression on all who heard it, that the God of the people who came out of Egypt was indeed a mighty God. This God would not only keep them from the sword of their enemies, but also hide them from the scourge of the tongue. The mighty prophet who had come to curse them could not say a word, except what the God of Israel put in his mouth.

Rahab, also, confessed without reserve to the messengers of Joshua, "The Lord your God, He is God in heaven above and in the earth beneath." She longed for their God to be her God. And so it happened, with Rahab actually being brought into the Messianic line.

And as the nation of the Israelites in Canaan grew greater and was brought more into contact with foreign powers, the influence of the truth that was among them was still more widely spread. One famous example occurs in the reign of the son of David. The Queen of Sheba came from the uttermost parts of the earth only at the report of Solomon. And if this report spread so far as Sheba on the south, why not equally far on the east, west, and north?

The story of the prophet Jonah is an illustration or how much truth might be brought to light in a ship with even one Hebrew on board.

But though it is easy to multiply these smaller illustrations, they are not the main thing. They do indeed show that there may have been far more effect on the world from the light that shone in the land of Israel than we are apt to think. But the most striking providential connection between Israel and the rest of the nations came through the captivity of Judah and Israel; of Judah especially, for with them went the priests and Levites and the Old Testament Scriptures, and the holy vessels of the temple of God.

The time chosen in God's providence to accomplish that captivity is very striking. It occurred at a most important crisis in the history of the world. We all know that it was Nebuchadnezzar who took Jerusalem and carried the tribe of Judah captive.

Nebuchadnezzar, the great king of Babylon, might be called the first licensed monarch of the whole ancient world. Let us refer to the terms of his license. "Thus saith the Lord of hosts the God of Israel: thus shall ye say unto your masters: I have made the earth, the man, and the beast that are upon the ground, by my great power and by my outstretched arm, and have given it unto whom it seemed meet unto Me. And now have I given all these lands into the hand of Nebuchadnezzar the king of Babylon, my servant; and the beasts of the field have I given him, also to serve him. And all nations shall serve him, and his son, and his son's son, until the very time of his land come, and then many nations and great kings shall serve themselves of him. And it shall come to pass, that the nation and kingdom which will not serve the same Nebuchadnezzar, the king of Babylon, and that will not put their neck under the yoke of the king of Babylon, that nation will I punish, saith the Lord, with the sword, and with the famine, and with the pestilence, until I have consumed them by his hand" (Jer. 27:4-9; see also Dan. 2:37-38).

There was a very definite plan and providence in the fact that this particular king was permitted in the beginning of his reign to seize God's ancient people and make them a subject race. Note also that he carried them to Babylon, to the very place where the Most High had

138

forcibly separated the sons of Adam nearly 1800 years before. He had separated them that they might not be one city or one kingdom, but many cities and many kingdoms, and that they might grow up separately, each with a character of its own. He reunited them at the same spot under one king (Nebuchadnezzar), that they might at last become one kingdom, if they could.

In that one kingdom, in the very heart of it, He placed His own chosen people with His written Word, so far as it was then completed, in order that they might be witnesses for Him. He even put into their mouth beforehand, in the language of their captors, the very words that they should use in asserting His divinity. "This shall ye say unto them: The gods that have not made the heavens and the earth, even they shall perish from the earth and from under these heavens" (see Jer. 10:11, which is found in the Chaldean language in the original). How His people did witness, the story of Daniel and of the three that walked in the fiery furnace remain to show. The effect may be seen in a decree of Nebuchadnezzar.

"Therefore I make a decree that every people, nation, and language which speak anything amiss against the God of Shadrach, Meshach, and Abed-nego shall be cut in pieces, and their houses made a dunghill: because there is no other God that can deliver after this sort" (Dan. 3:29).

From this point in history (about 600 BC), we may say that the times of the Gentiles begin. The connection between God's chosen people and the great Gentile powers, when once established, was never broken off. They were under Nebuchadnezzar and Darius at Babylon. Cyrus, the Persian, sent them back to their own city, but they were a part of his kingdom throughout his reign. Ezra, and Nehemiah, and Queen Esther, and Mordecai were all witnesses, not to their own people merely, but to the Gentiles also, witnesses for the truth of God. When the Persian kingdom had given place to that of Alexander, and the empire that he had conquered was broken into four heads, there arose a translation of the Old Testament Scriptures in the Greek tongue, the language then spoken throughout the whole of the civilized world.

These are the familiar facts of history, but they go far to establish the point. The connection between the Israelites and these nations of old, from first to last, was providential. And when the greatest kingdom of the ancient world was established in its strength; (and perhaps there has never been a more widely extended government of equal strength as ancient Rome), this mighty empire appropriated all that had been developed by the kingdoms that were before, and the Jews were dispersed from one end to the other of the known world.

Wherever the apostles went to preach, they must have found the Jewish synagogues and the Greek translation of the Old Testament Scriptures as a foundation upon which to work. And so it was that the world was first evangelized in a great measure by the use of a machinery which belonged to the Jews.

Thus we see that each of the four empires had its fair opportunity in the way most suitable to itself. The despotisms of Babylon and Persia had their opportunity through their kings, Greece through its language and thought. Rome reduced Judea to a province in the lifetime of our Lord (the greatest Israelite that ever lived), and after 300 years of conflict with Christianity, the entire empire yielded itself to the gospel (or at least to Christendom). Each and all of these universal empires had the offer of that wonderful religion whose pattern was in the heavens, whose law was in the very handwriting of the Most High.

Let us not say that these opportunities were small. Let us rather remind ourselves that the least ray of light is enough to prove whether light or darkness is preferred. "He that is faithful in that which is least, is faithful also in much, and he that is unjust in least, is unjust also in much" (Lk. 16:10). If a small opportunity is rejected, it is not necessary that God should give another. It is not essential to His justice, though He may bestow it out of the fullness of His love.

But the truth regarding Israel is only half before us as yet. What shall the receiving of them be to the Gentiles, but life from the dead? So it is quite significant that the names of the tribes of Israel are written above the gates of the Golden City. "Whosoever will enter must pass under the name of one of the twelve tribes." Whosoever will "seek the Lord," and find Him does so as a result of the promise of God to Abraham, that through his Seed all nations would be blessed. The Word of God and the Son of God came through the Israelite nation. But throughout history, the faithful (and sometimes unfaithful) ones in Israel, knowingly or ignorantly, were a testimony to the reality of "the Most High. "When the Most High divided to the nations their inheritance, when He separated the sons of Adam, He set the bounds of the people according to the number of the children of Israel. For the Lord's portion is His people. Jacob is the lot of His inheritance" (Deut. 32:8-9).

MAPS

143

THE TRIBAL
TERRITORIES
GIVEN TO
JACOB'S
SONS

Tyre
Dan
EAST
MANASSEH
ASHER
NAPHTALI
Capernaum
ZEBULUN
Sea of
Galilee
Golan
Nazareth
ISSACHAR
Jezreel
Mediterranean
Sea
MANASSEH
Jabesh-gilead
Jordan River
Samaria
Joppa
Shiloh
GAD
DAN EPHRAIM
Ammon
BENJAMIN
Jerusalem
Mt. Nebo
Bethlehem
JUDAH
REUBEN
Dead
Sea
Beersheba
Moab
SIMEON

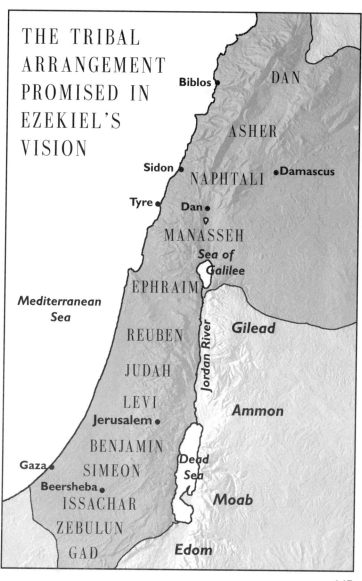

THE TRIBAL
ARRANGEMENT
PROMISED IN
EZEKIEL'S
VISION

Biblos

DAN

ASHER

Sidon

NAPHTALI

•Damascus

Tyre

Dan

MANASSEH

Sea of
Galilee

EPHRAIM

Mediterranean
Sea

REUBEN

Jordan River

Gilead

JUDAH

LEVI

Jerusalem •

Ammon

BENJAMIN

Dead
Sea

Gaza

SIMEON

Beersheba

ISSACHAR

Moab

ZEBULUN

GAD

Edom

SCRIPTURE INDEX